Colin Wilson achieved sudden best-sellerdom with his first book *The Outsider*, a study of alienated individuals, in 1956, when he was 24. His first novel, *Ritual in the Dark*, was based on the Jack the Ripper murders. In 1961, *An Encyclopaedia of Murder* (with Pat Pitman) was published. Since then he has published works on philosophy, psychology, the paranormal (*The Occult*, 1971, was a bestseller) and criminology. The latter include *A Criminal History of Mankind*, *Written in Blood* (the history of forensic detection), *The Serial Killers* (with Donald Seaman) and *A Plague of Murder* (history of serial killers.) He has been an editor of the partworks *Crime and Punishment*, *Murder Casebook* and *Murder in Mind*.

The complete
TRUE CRIME LIBRARY

A NEW CENTURY OF SEX KILLERS
FATAL ATTRACTION
A DATE WITH THE HANGMAN
MURDER WITH VENOM
BRITAIN'S GODFATHER
ON DEATH ROW
WOMEN ON DEATH ROW
BEDSIDE BOOK OF MURDER
LOVE YOU TO DEATH
STRANGE TALES FROM STRANGEWAYS
DIARY OF A HANGMAN
FROM WALL STREET TO NEWGATE
CAMINADA THE CRIMEBUSTER
FROM THE X-FILES OF MURDER
FAR FROM THE LAND
THE CORPSE GARDEN
THE BOOTLEGGERS
CLASSIC MURDERS OF THE NORTH EAST

THE CORPSE GARDEN

The Crimes of
Fred and Rose West

Colin Wilson

PAN BOOKS

First published 1998 by True Crime Library

This edition published 2003 by Pan Books
an imprint of Pan Macmillan Ltd
Pan Macmillan, 20 New Wharf Road, London N1 99R
Basingstoke and Oxford
Associated companies throughout the world
www.panmacmillan.com

ISBN 0 330 42104 2

3 5 7 9 8 6 4 2

A CIP catalogue record for this book is available from
the British Library.

Printed and bound in Great Britain by
Mackays of Chatham plc, Chatham, Kent

CONTENTS

Introduction

The Fred West case is arguably the worst case of serial murder in British criminal history. It is true that the homosexual Dennis Nilsen, who murdered fifteen young men at his north London flats between 1978 and 1983, exceeded West's total of victims by three; but he simply strangled them when they were drunk, then kept their bodies in his flat "for company" before dismembering them. In the Moors murder case Ian Brady, aided by his lover Myra Hindley, abducted four children and one youth of seventeen and murdered them, but in spite of lurid stories of torture there is no evidence that the motivation was anything but paedophilia. But Frederick West and his wife Rose went further than either; they abducted girls, then subjected them to sadistic sex, hanging them from a beam, after binding tape around their faces until they looked like mummies, with only glass tubes inserted in the nostrils so they could breathe. When the remains were unearthed missing fingers and toes suggested even worse excesses.

Ever since 1963, when I wrote a book called *Origins of the Sexual Impulse*, I have been puzzled and intrigued by the way that "normal" sexual desire can turn into sadism. For example, the American serial killer Ted Bundy (executed in January 1989) began his career of rape and murder when he glimpsed a woman getting undressed through a lighted window, and became an obsessive Peeping Tom. This led him to kidnap and rape. But this in turn developed into torturing his victims — he later admitted that what he did to his final victim, 12-year-old Kim Leach, was so horrible that he could not bring himself to describe it.

Now any normal male can understand how a man could be so excited by watching a woman undress that he becomes a rapist. But most of us find it virtually impossible to understand how rape can turn into torture.

Kenneth Bianchi and Angelo Buono, the "Hillside Stranglers" of Los Angeles, developed their taste for violation after murdering a prostitute against whom they had a grudge, and deciding that they might as well rape her too. They found this so enjoyable that they began to lure women to Buono's house to rape and then murder them — on one occasion, two schoolgirls. Soon they were deriving most of their pleasure from suffocating the women with a plastic bag, allowing them to breathe again, then suffocating them again.

Perhaps the worst case of all is that of "Pee Wee" Gaskins, executed in 1991. Gaskins had committed his first rape in his teens, when he and two friends lured the 13-year-old sister of one of them to their "hideaway", and spent the afternoon raping and sodomising her. She begged them to stop "but we just couldn't ... It was too good." After later being sent to prison for raping another underage girl, Gaskins decided that in future he would kill his rape victims. This decision released a torrent of sadism that even Gaskins had not suspected existed within him. He often tortured his victims (he estimated more than a hundred of them) with boiling lead. On one occasion he ate a girl over the course of three days while she was still alive. Even Gaskins admitted that he was one of the most evil men who ever existed. A writer named Wilton Earle, who wrote down Gaskins' life story — in his own words — in prison was so nauseated that he had a nervous breakdown, and believes that a cancer he later developed was the result of the trauma of listening to these appalling accounts of torture.

It would be simple and convenient to explain Gaskins as a "mental case", a freak, an exception to the human rule. But dozens of similar cases make it clear that Gaskins was not an exception. His sadism may have gone a great deal further than that of others — even Fred West — but it followed the same course, like some illness whose stages are predictable. His case makes it clear that indulgence in inflicting pain becomes obsessive and addictive.

The beginning of an explanation would seem to lie in the fact that the male sexual impulse is predatory by nature: a desire to "use" a woman for the satisfaction of a sexual itch, and that it depends on desire for "the forbidden." The mechanism has been described by Mark Twain in *Tom Sawyer*, in the chapter where Tom has been ordered to spend his Saturday morning whitewashing a fence. But when a friend stops by to jeer at him Tom whistles, and looks as if he is enjoying it so much that the friend asks him if he can whitewash for five minutes. Soon Tom has a queue waiting for their turn, while he lies back and takes his ease.

Twain reflects that "in order to make a man or a boy covet a thing, it is only necessary to make the thing difficult to attain." Nature has hit upon the device of making men covet women by making them difficult to attain. So if a woman combines physical attractiveness with a demure manner that suggests that even the thought of sex would make her blush, she will have a permanent queue of admirers waiting to whitewash the fence.

Now the simplest form of this urge is the desire to kiss. The actress Florence Farr used to get so bored with young men gazing longingly at her mouth that she used to seize them by the ears, give them a kiss, then say: "That's got that over — now let's have a reasonable conversation." But kissing is essentially a gesture of affection — after all, Florence Farr did not expect her admirers to bite her. The same is true of sexual intercourse, which is why we use the euphemism "lovemaking." The question is: how can "lovemaking" turn into a desire to inflict pain?

Part of the answer obviously lies in male aggression: after all, the act of penetrating a woman is a kind of aggression, and passionate lovemaking is often violent. But even that fails to explain how a woman like Rose West can also become addicted to torture — to terrifying members of her own sex, and finally taking part in their murder.

What I am trying to pinpoint is the phenomenology of sadism. The reader should not be alarmed by the word phenomenology. It means merely putting yourself in the place of someone — in this case, a sadist — trying to see the world through his eyes, and describing what you observe.

I stumbled upon an interesting clue in reading a book about the Manson "family." Susan Atkins, who participated in the Manson murders, describes how the first time she had sex with Charles Manson he told her to imagine that he was her father. The result, she says, was one of the most exciting sexual experiences of her life.

Why should that be? The average daughter would feel rather shocked at the idea of sex with her father. And this is precisely why she found it so exciting. It involved overcoming a certain inhibition. An inhibition involves flinching away from something, in the way a bather flinches away from putting a foot into cold water. Overcoming an inhibition requires an act of will, which involves summoning energy. If you walk into cold water on a hot day, each step involves a twinge of discomfort — yet this discomfort increases the pleasure. Your resistance to the cold water increases your energy. Through this increase in energy, the mind has the capacity to somehow turn discomfort into pleasure.

It is a paradox, but that is the way our pleasure mechanism works. Scratching yourself when you itch is a pleasure that has an element of pain — and the pain is pleasant. Pain can be transmuted into pleasure, as every masochist knows.

So the idea that it was her father who was making love to her aroused in Susan Atkins a resistance which was swept away by sexual excitement. And the process of sweeping away the inhibition actually added to the sexual excitement by adding an element of "naughtiness", of "forbiddenness." Her mind transformed the negative into the positive — the same mechanism that makes surfing in a rough sea more exhilarating than surfing in a calm sea.

Most imaginative people have had this experience of using the force of resistance to increase pleasure. An adolescent, seething with erotic energy, looks around for forbidden objects of desire. Left alone in the house, he gets the medical book out of its locked cupboard, or looks through his mother's magazines for pictures of women in their underwear; perhaps, like Roth's Portnoy, he gets his sister's knickers out of the laundry basket. When talking to the girl next door, he wonders what she would think if she knew that he has just been raping her in his imagination.

The stronger the sexual desire, the more "forbidden" the act of imagination needed to satisfy it. The Düsseldorf sadist Peter Kürten, beheaded in 1931, told the psychiatrist Karl Berg that his sadism had developed while he was in solitary confinement in prison, indulging in lurid sexual fantasies. The fantasies finally became so violent that when he came out of prison he could not make love to his wife without imagining that he was cutting off her head. He was using the same "principle of resistance" as Susan Atkins, deliberately breaking down his inhibitions, as he might chop up furniture to feed a fire.

Now the problem is that inhibitions are social in nature. A teenager may rape the girl next door in imagination, but if he really wants to make love to her he has to gain her consent. Even raping her in imagination demands the breaking down of a certain inhibition — which is why he may blush if he actually speaks to her, and remembers what he was imagining just five minutes ago.

This explains why Pee Wee Gaskins was startled at the flood of sadism that overwhelmed him when he decided to murder his rape victims. There was a sense in which the decision to kill the girl transferred the act from the realm of reality to the realm of imagination. The difference between imagination and reality is that in the realm of reality we have to take account of other people, while in the realm of imagination we can do what we like. His decision to murder the girl meant that he no longer had to take account of her as a person. In effect, she had become a character in his fantasy.

This also explains why the Hillside Stranglers

became addicted to murder after killing and raping a prostitute. The decision to kill her meant that the "social" element, the element of mutual interaction, had been removed from sex. They were turning it into a totally subjective experience, and releasing their inhibitions like releasing a pack of guard dogs.

This certainly goes a long way towards explaining the psychology of sadism. Yet it still fails to explain how the desire to inflict pain can actually replace the desire for normal intercourse. Fred West told his son Stephen, who visited him in prison, that he did not make love to the girls until after they were dead. That sounds absurd. The obvious reason for kidnapping a girl is to have sex without her consent. Yet in West's case rape had become a kind of afterthought. How can we explain that paradox?

This brings us to what, it seems to me, is the most important insight of all: that all our greatest pleasures are associative. I have only to smell a kind of sweetmeat called candyfloss — which is sold at fairgrounds — to be carried back to childhood days at the seaside. I have only to smell cut grass after my lawn has been mowed to be reminded of the smell of new-mown hay in the countryside. In the same way, a man who loves food and wine not only enjoys eating and drinking; he also enjoys reading books about food and wine, and talking about it with other gourmets. A man who loves travel also enjoys television programmes about travel, and books with colour photographs of distant places.

What is even more paradoxical is that a man may enjoy a television programme about travel more than the travel itself. After all, when you are in a strange town you are there and nowhere else, and it is not so different from being at home. But when you are in an armchair watching a television programme — particularly about some place you have visited — you are in two places at once: your own sitting-room, and the other side of the world.

Sex is the most associative of all pleasures. Every sexual experience of our lives — and that means imaginative as well as real experience — leaves its mark on us. And sexual imagination is so strong that a book or a picture can arouse as much excitement as sex itself. A character in Kingsley Amis' *Girl Twenty* remarks that even the words "Girl, twenty" in an advertisement can give him an erection. Medical textbooks are full of cases of men who associate their first sexual arousal with fur or the smell of sour milk, and thereafter experience sexual excitement every time they touch fur or smell sour milk.

But now we come to the real paradox: that something as explosive as sexual excitement can nevertheless become a matter of habit. But then that applies to all our pleasures. We discover some new product in the supermarket, and become addicted to it. Then our taste buds become accustomed to its flavour, and our interest fades. In the same way a honeymoon couple may find an excuse to hurry off to their bedroom half a dozen times a day; but after a month or so sex has taken its place among the many other routines of their lives. They still enjoy it, but it no longer has quite the same power to excite the imagination. Sex, like every other pleasure, can become mechanical.

But this is not always so. Freud was fascinated by the case of a man called Ivan Poderjay, which he described as the most complex case of polymorphous perversion that he had ever encountered. Poderjay and his wife played an endless series of sexual games. Sometimes she was the helpless victim, he the sadistic tyrant. Sometimes he was the woman, she was the man. Sometimes she was the dominatrix, and he was her disobedient lapdog. Poderjay eventually met his downfall after murdering a woman and slicing her body to pieces with razor blades; there can be no doubt that he chose this peculiar method of disposal because it gave him pleasure. But while their relationship lasted, he and his wife certainly found many ways of preventing it from settling into boring routine.

Fred and Rose West had also found ways of preventing their sex lives from degenerating into routine. Both regarded sex as the most important thing in life. Rose told a friend that when she retired from motherhood she meant to devote the rest of her days to sex. From the moment they met, life became a continual sexual orgy. Rose was a nymphomaniac, who had no objection when Fred brought other men home, and watched while they satisfied her.

But Rose liked women as much as men, so it was important that some of their sex partners should be women. And since both were bondage enthusiasts, they enjoyed tying up their sexual partners or taping them down to the bed. They ended by killing some of them — either in the throes of sexual excitement, or to prevent the victim from telling what had happened.

They soon discovered, like the Hillside Stranglers, that rape that involves the death of the victim was intensely addictive. Inflicting pain had ceased to be the means to an end, and had become the end in itself.

Like the case of Ivan Poderjay, the case of Fred and Rose West is one of the strangest in the history of polymorphous perversion.

When I was about ten years old I once spent the afternoon playing with a friend who showed me how to turn small dragonflies into "aeroplanes" by pulling them in half and inserting a tiny piece of stick in them, then throwing them. After half an hour I felt oddly sick and disgusted, and never played the game again. Most normal people, I believe, feel a similar inhibition about gratuitous killing.

1
RAPE

Gloucester is the kind of place that often gets left out of the guide books. It was once a Roman city, and a seat of English kings; at least three of its dukes figure in Shakespeare's plays. But in the 20th century it has turned into a typical modern city with little to distinguish it; the young are bored and dissatisfied, there is a high level of crime and vandalism, and drug addicts hang out in the local parks.

Even for students of crime, Gloucester has no great interest: unlike most British cities, it has had no famous murders, unless you count the horrible demise of King Edward II in 1327, killed by the insertion of a red hot iron into his rectum, in a castle ten miles away.

This must immediately be qualified by saying that its criminal record was undistinguished until 1994, when the crimes of Fred West brought Gloucester a sudden and spectacular notoriety. For West is almost certainly the worst serial killer that Britain has produced so far, in his methods of operation and — probably — the number of his victims.

Cromwell Street is a narrow road of Victorian houses, within a few hundred yards of the main railway station in central Gloucester. It is not a "good" area — police are often called there to intervene in domestic disputes and brawls. To their neighbours the Wests who lived in number 25 seemed a perfectly normal couple; it was a three-storey, semi-detached house that was crammed with children and teenage lodgers. Fred West was a swarthy, slightly simian-looking man with long side-burns, piercing blue eyes, and a gap between his front teeth. He seemed to spend most of his spare time dressed in overalls and a builder's protective helmet, adding various extensions to his house. His wife Rosemary, twelve years her husband's junior, was plump, bespectacled and plain. To her friends she was known as Rose, to her family as Rosie.

A few neighbours may have noticed the unusual number of male callers, many of them black, and the fact that two of the younger daughters were half-castes, but then since most of the surrounding houses were full of bedsits, no one was curious enough to pay them much attention.

Then, one day in late May, 1992, life in 25 Cromwell Street changed forever.

Rose West had gone out shopping, leaving her husband at home with the five younger children, four girls and a boy, whose ages ranged from 9 to 16. The children were watching television when West asked one of the girls to make him a cup of tea, then asked another to bring some bottles up to the bar on the first floor. He followed her into the room, and locked the door.

Inside the room, he posed the girl on the settee, pointed a video camera at her, then undressed her and raped her. Then, in spite of her cries, he turned her over and sodomised her, after which he raped her again. He was clearly in a state of fevered sexual excitement.

Hearing the screams of "No, don't, dad," one of

the younger sisters went upstairs and knocked on the door. West's angry voice shouted: "What do you fucking want?" The child said: "Your tea's ready, dad." A few minutes later West, scowling angrily, came downstairs.

One of the children asked if she could go upstairs to see her sister. West replied brusquely: "She's busy." But the girl took the first opportunity to slip upstairs. She found her sister crying and writhing in pain, repeating: "He hurt me, he hurt me." She described how her father had raped her, using a lubricant but no condom, and how at one point he had grabbed her round the throat and squeezed until she thought she was going to die. He had even videotaped the rape.

As soon as her mother came home the girl told her what had happened. Rose West shrugged. "Oh well, you were asking for it." She was not the kind of mother to take the side of her children against her husband.

During the next few days West raped his daughter again, explaining that it might cause medical problems if he did not "finish the job properly." The following day he took her to a warehouse he was painting near Reading, and raped her again.

When Mae, one of the Wests' elder daughters, learned about the rape she decided something had to be done about it. Mae was not in the least surprised by her mother's lack of concern. She herself had been raped at the age of 8 — in 1980 — not by her father, but by a male visitor to the house, who had taken her into the bathroom, laid her on a board covering the bath, and ordered her to stop wriggling as he penetrated her; afterwards he gave her 10 pence and told her not to tell anyone. Most children would have run to their parents, but Mae knew that it would be a waste of time. At 25 Cromwell Street the atmosphere of sexuality was like a heavy fog; her father seldom talked of anything else. She had no doubt that if she told him she had been raped Fred West would say: "Oh, that's all right — he's a friend."

The day after the rape of her sister, Mae went to call on her half-sister Anne Marie, the daughter of West's first wife Rena, who was eight years her senior. Anne Marie had left home when she was 15 because her father had made her pregnant. Now, when Mae told her what had happened, Anne-Marie asked her if she could steal the videotape, so they could use it as evidence. Mae promised she would try.

When Mae had gone Anne Marie called a child-protection charity called Childline, set up to help children who are being sexually abused. But Childline explained that the victim of the rape would have to phone them herself before they could act.

A few days later the victim told a schoolfriend what had happened, and on August 2, 1992, the friend mentioned it to a policeman with whom she was talking, and he reported it. It was not the first time that the Gloucester police had heard rumours of child abuse in the West household, but they had never been able to accumulate definite evidence. They had also had occasion to question Fred West about theft, and now they decided to call at his home on the pretext of investigating stolen goods.

Early in the morning on August 6, 1992, they made a thorough search, and found an extraordinary assortment of sex aids, including whips, dildos, rubber suits, chains, handcuffs, ninety-nine pornographic videos — several showing Rose West having sex with other men — and a huge collection of hard-porn magazines. The police took these away. But they did not find what they were hoping for — the video showing the rape of the daughter.

When the policemen came to the door Rose West's first reaction had been to order all the children to go to their bedrooms — she wanted to make sure that the police had no opportunity to speak to them. Fred West went off to work while the search was still going on. Rose was placed under arrest just after 9 a.m., and taken to the police station for questioning. Fred West was arrested at work, and questioned about the rape of his daughter. He was kept in custody; Rose was allowed to go home after twenty-four hours. When Rose returned to 25 Cromwell Street the first thing she did was to tell Mae — who had been looking after the younger children — to leave the house, in case the police questioned her.

Early the next morning the police arrived again, this time with social workers to take the children into care. When Rose became angry and abusive, and pushed a policewoman downstairs, the police grabbed her and twisted her arm behind her back; she was arrested for the second time in two days. The charge was assault, and neglecting the children. She was soon allowed to go home, but her husband remained in custody.

When Rose came home alone she was quiet and subdued. With the younger children in care, she seemed oddly disoriented. Mae and her younger brother Stephen, who had been living away from home, decided to move in with her. A few evenings later she came into the living-room looking dazed, and called out Stephen's name, then collapsed on the settee, mumbling incoherently. Wondering if she was drunk, he went to check the bar, but could see no sign of an empty glass. Then he went into her bedroom, and found an empty box of Anadin tablets.

Forty-eight seemed to be missing. He sent for an ambulance, and Rose was taken to hospital to have her stomach pumped out. When she came home she seemed old and frail.

The children who had been taken into care had been medically examined; the examination revealed that more than one of them had been the victim of some kind of sexual interference. And the daughter who had been raped had made a full statement to a solicitor. Mae accompanied her mother when she went to see him, and listened as he read it aloud. It was clear that Fred West felt that in effect his daughter had now become his mistress, and that he intended to continue having sex with her on a regular basis.

As she listened, Mae realised that it could just as easily have been her own name on the bottom of the statement. Her father had often said to his daughters: "I made you — I can do what I like with you." When they were fairly young, he had told them that he intended to deflower them as soon as they were old enough. It was, he explained, a father's duty — for if some inexperienced youth did it clumsily, it might cause "medical problems."

Throughout her teens, Mae had succeeded in avoiding rape, although her father liked to walk into the bathroom when she was in the shower, and reach around the curtain to caress her. He did not seem to regard this as a sexual advance — merely as his right to inspect something that was his own property. She had stopped wearing a skirt, since her father was unable to resist putting his hand up it, so she made a habit of changing into jeans as soon as she returned from school. Even then West would raise her blouse, remove her bra, and fondle her breasts. On one occasion, with Rose in the room, he had wrestled her to the floor, and when she screamed in alarm her mother had told her not to be silly — her father was only playing.

This had been going on for years. Mae and her elder sister Heather had waited for their father to go out, or stood guard for one another, before they took a shower or undressed for bed. Their father had drilled holes in the wall of their bedroom so he could watch them undressing; but at least he would not attempt rape with two of them present. But now Heather had gone away — the Wests claimed she had run away with a lesbian — and they had not heard from her in four years.

The woman policeman who was dealing with the case was Detective Constable Hazel Savage, a calm, efficient woman in her late forties, who had held her present rank for twenty-four years. A divorcee, she wore her hair cut short, and horn-rimmed spectacles. She had first seen Fred West twenty-six years earlier, in 1966 — he had appeared in court as a witness when his first wife Rena was charged with burglary. Hazel Savage had also been sent to Scotland to collect Rena, and recalled that the girl told her that her husband was a sexual pervert who was probably insane ...

Now Hazel Savage went to call on the Wests' eldest daughter Anne Marie — the one who had left home at fifteen after her father had made her pregnant. And when she told Anne Marie what the rape victim had said in her statement, and that Fred West was denying the whole thing, Anne Marie came to a difficult decision — to tell for the first time what had happened to her. Hazel Savage took her back to the police station, and there, fortified by endless cups of tea and cigarettes, Anne Marie told the whole story. She found it so traumatic that it took most of the day.

As a child, Anne Marie had adored her father; she

called herself "daddy's girl", and often said that she would marry him when she grew up. She disliked her step-mother, because Rose was bad-tempered, and often beat the children, but she never had cause to be afraid of her father — at least, until that summer evening in 1973, when Anne Marie was eight years old, and Fred and Rose led her down to the basement, tied her hands together, and deflowered her with a vibrator. When finally they let her go she was hardly able to walk, but Rose seemed to find it funny.

For a few weeks they left her to heal up. But as soon as that happened they resumed the sexual abuse. It was clear that Rose found it as exciting as her husband.

When, a few weeks later, Anne Marie turned nine, West began having sexual intercourse with her.

Fred West was a voyeur. Ever since their first days together, he had insisted that Rose should go to bed with other men while he watched — they were often his mates from work. Now the thought that his daughter was no longer a virgin was obviously a source of tremendous excitement to him. He constructed a device that would hold the vibrator in place with a strap about her waist and made her wear it as she walked around the house. And on one occasion, when he had been watching Rose having sex with one of her black lovers, he took a condom full of semen, tied it at the end, and made her wear it inside her as she watched television.

All this — and much more — Anne Marie described to Detective Constable Hazel Savage during that long afternoon. She also told her that she was worried about her half-sister Heather, who had vanished from home in May 1987. Anne Marie had been to Devon looking for her — at the time of leaving home, Heather was due to start a job at a holiday camp in Torquay — and had also contacted the Samaritans, a group who specialise in helping the severely depressed. But no one had seen her sister. Hazel Savage promised that she would try and find Heather.

Fred West was now in Gloucester prison on remand. His eldest son Stephen went to see him there, and found him a changed man. While not normally violent, Fred West seemed to go insane when he lost his temper, and could leave his children battered and bleeding. Now, suddenly, he had become gentler, and often cried. He told Stephen that he had done stupid things while the children were asleep in bed, and committed the worst crime they could imagine. Stephen found it hard to guess what he was talking about. But when he thought about the disappearance of his sister Heather, he began to wonder ...

Alone at 25 Cromwell Street, Rose West had also changed. So far she had supported her husband in everything he did. Now he had caused the loss of her children, she seemed to have her first serious doubts. She broke with the Jamaican lover who had fathered three of her children, and gave up other extra-marital involvements. It was clear that she felt that something had come to an end, and that her husband was to blame. He had been in prison before — for theft — but this time it looked as if he would be inside for a long time. And so, quite possibly, would she, if Anne Marie told her story in court.

Without her husband's income, Rose West was forced to take a job as a cleaner. She acquired two dogs from a rescue centre, but showed little capacity for dealing with animals — when they annoyed her, she beat them brutally. She spent a great deal of time watching cartoons on television, often naked, eating cream chocolates.

The evidence against Fred West seemed watertight; with detailed signed statements from two of his children, it should have been impossible for him to escape conviction. Yet, strangely enough, the victim of his latest rape was unwilling to press charges. When Mae went to see her, she told Mae that she was hoping to be allowed home. Stephen went even further in trying to protect his father — he told the police that he had committed the rape, but they had no doubt he was lying.

The truth was that although 25 Cromwell Street had never been an ideal home for children, it was all they had — it represented all their security. Suddenly placed in care, forbidden to see their mother, they felt lonely and insecure — they even sneaked back to visit Cromwell Street.

Aware of the unhappiness of her brothers and sisters, Anne Marie began to feel that perhaps she ought to to change her story. Besides, she was afraid for her own two children — she knew how vindictive Rose could be. This was why she finally decided to give way and withdraw her statement. About two months after she had made it, she told Hazel Savage that it was all invention.

Hazel Savage said: "Look at me and tell me it isn't true."

Anne Marie turned her head away. "I made it all up."

Hazel Savage warned her that she could be charged with wasting police time. But she had no real intention of making Anne Marie's life difficult. She was still hoping for her co-operation in bringing Fred and Rose West to justice.

Fred and Rose West were apart for nearly a year.

The case finally came to court on June 17, 1993, when they stood side by side in the dock — Fred charged with raping and buggering his daughter, and Rose with inciting him to have sex with her. The case lasted only a few minutes. Since the victim refused to testify, Fred and Rose West were able to walk out of court. West was relieved and delighted. Back at home, he flung his arms around Mae, and told her that their troubles were over, and that life could now return to normal.

But it was not true. The younger children were not allowed to return to Cromwell Street. The Social Services offered to allow them to come for supervised visits, but the Wests refused   they felt suspicious and hostile towards social workers. But without the family the house seemed bare and empty.

West was furious to discover that his pornographic tapes and magazines had vanished, and that Rose had returned even the video camera, which was on hire purchase. He not only demanded that they should start collecting porn again, but that Rose should begin offering her services in sex magazines: "Sexy housewife wants well-endowed males — husband likes to watch." But Rose flatly refused. She was finished with all that. Ever since she had been a fifteen-year-old schoolgirl she had allowed Fred's will to prevail. Now it had ruined their lives, it was time to call a halt. And since Rose was the stronger of the two characters, Fred reluctantly accepted her verdict. He even made no protest when she gave the police permission to destroy the videos that they had seized.

He told Stephen and Mae that Heather had visited him at the Carpenter House Bail Hostel in Birmingham, and that she would soon be home. Heather had become a prostitute, he said, and was earning lots of money. He also claimed that he had seen her at a certain hostel in Gloucester. Mae went there, hoping to see her sister, but soon realised that her father had been lying.

In fact both Stephen and Mae now suspected that Heather had been murdered by their parents. They recalled all their unsuccessful efforts to contact their sister, and how when they told their father that they were going to the police to report her missing he had made them sit down, and explained that Heather had been involved in credit card frauds, and would be arrested if she was found. And they recalled something else — that their father had often joked that Heather was buried underneath the patio.

WPC Savage had heard the same story — it was repeated to her by the couple who were now fostering the younger children. One of the boys had mentioned that their father threatened to beat them black and blue if they ever talked about what went on in the house, and that they would end up under the patio, like their sister Heather. It seemed an odd kind of threat to make. Hazel Savage decided to call on Anne Marie again. And Anne Marie confirmed that it was a family joke — the first time her father had made it, sitting at the kitchen table, he had roared with laughter, obviously finding it very funny. Recalling his laughter, Anne Marie found it impossible to believe that it had been intended seriously.

Hazel Savage was not convinced. With the aid of the social services, she had been trying to trace Heather West. If she was working, then she must have a Social Security number, and pay tax. But neither the Social Security department nor the Inland Revenue could find any trace of her. Her total disappearance suggested that she was dead, and probably buried underneath the patio at 25 Cromwell Street — a patio West had laid after her disappearance.

The Wests also knew that Hazel Savage was looking for Heather. They pretended to treat it as a joke, and Fred assured everybody that the charges against him had been concocted by Hazel Savage in pursuance of a vendetta. Now they were back together again, Fred and Rose had become very close, and often sat holding hands on the settee. A psychologist who had assessed them before the trial had described them as a loving couple, with no secrets from one another. Now they even decided to start another family, and Rose went to the local hospital to try to have an earlier sterilisation reversed. It worked, and she became pregnant again — but this was soon followed by a miscarriage.

That winter after the trial, the Wests seemed to want to isolate themselves. They had never been a particularly sociable couple, even to the extent of being rude to their children's schoolfriends. Now they seemed to want to cut off contact with everybody. Rose's younger brother Graham and his wife Barbara — who had been Rose's closest friends for years — were banned from the house. The rest of their relatives had given them up years ago — Rose's sister had been scandalised when Fred tried to persuade her that she and her husband ought to try wife-swopping. And since the death of Fred's father and mother, he had lost contact with most of his own brothers and sisters. Life at Cromwell Street became increasingly lonely.

Hazel Savage had been trying hard to convince her superiors that they ought to investigate the patio at 25 Cromwell Street. Her boss was dubious. To begin with, the Wests might claim harassment after the previous attempt to prosecute them, and have grounds for suing the police. Digging up the garden would be expensive; West had covered it with concrete slabs, and built an extension on part of it; this might have to be demolished. All this would attract the attention of the press, and if they found nothing the Gloucester Police Department would look foolish.

But Hazel Savage's persistence finally paid off. She was held in high esteem, and had many past successes to her credit. So on Wednesday, February 23, 1994, the Gloucester police applied for a warrant to search 25 Cromwell Street for the remains of Heather West. Detective Superintendent John Bennett was placed in charge.

The following day at about 1 o'clock, four policemen and a policewoman arrived at 25 Cromwell Street. It was Mae who opened the door. When they told her that they had a warrant to search for the body of Heather West, she was shocked. There had been a time when she and Stephen had discussed the possibility that their father had murdered Heather, but they had finally agreed that it was unlikely. Now the certainty with which the police talked about a body revived all Mae's fears.

The police walked in without asking, and presented the warrant to Rose West. She read it without speaking, then said angrily: "This is stupid." Rose had always hated the police.

She turned to her son Stephen. "Get Fred!"

But it proved unexpectedly difficult. He was replacing the timbers in the roof of a house near Stroud, and failed to answer his mobile phone. Finally, almost two hours after the police had arrived, Stephen reached him while he was driving. Stephen expected him to explode with rage when told that the police were already digging up his back garden, but he sounded curiously calm. He asked after Rose, said "Tell her I'll be home soon", and rang off.

By now the police were tearing up the patio slabs, and had taken down the garden fence so they could move away the barrowloads of earth. It suddenly came home to Stephen that they really expected to find a body. He still found the idea absurd.

Rose had calmed down, and looked as if she was in shock. She kept on asking what had happened to Fred. It should have taken him only half an hour to get home, yet now it was more than two hours since he had spoken to his son. No one has ever established what West did that afternoon instead of returning home; in the light of later developments, it seems possible that he drove to some unknown destination to make sure that some other secret was still secure.

It was a cold, gloomy winter day, and by 4 o'clock darkness was beginning to fall. The diggers switched on arc lamps plugged in to the Wests' electricity supply. But by the time Fred West arrived home, shortly before 6 o'clock, the searchers had left, leaving a policemen to guard the back garden.

Fred West went to the police station to make a statement. By now he was in an aggressive mood, and accused the police of harassment. And although no one had accused him of killing Heather, West stated unprompted that he had not murdered her. He even repeated the statement to a reporter he met outside the police station.

Back at Cromwell Street, Rose was being interviewed by two police officers in the first-floor room that served as a bar. She claimed not to know what had happened to Heather — she said she had been out shopping, and that when she returned Heather had left. She was reminded that she had earlier claimed that she had given Heather £600 to help her start a new life, and asked which bank account she had drawn it from. Again she became abusive and foul-mouthed. "I can't fucking remember ... What do you think I am, a bloody computer?" But she declared that Heather was a difficult and obstinate child, and that they had never been on close terms.

She explained that she thought Heather was a lesbian; asked why she thought so, she explained that even when Heather was at infant school, she knew exactly what kind of knickers the teacher had on.

Fred returned home when the interviewers had left. Stephen and Mae were still there. From the window they could see the light at the bottom of the garden, where a policeman was guarding the hole and reading a book; the night was icy cold. The only thing that seemed to worry Fred West was whether the police would discover that he had bypassed his electricity meter so that he would get free electricity.

At first daylight, the diggers were back again. As Stephen was about to leave for work, Fred West said suddenly: "Look, son, look after your mum and Mae. I'm going away for a bit." Stephen asked why. "I've done something really bad. Go to the papers and make as much money as you can." He stared out of the window at the diggers, and when he turned towards Stephen again his face was contorted with rage. Speaking of his expression, Stephen said later: "It definitely wasn't normal."

Hazel Savage came soon after, and when she asked Rose how she could get in touch with her mother Rose flew into a rage. Fred led her out of the room, then came back and told the police he was willing to go with them. It was at this point that he was charged with the murder of his daughter Heather. As West left the house — photographed by a crowd of reporters — he was bellowing: "I didn't kill my daughter." Neighbours came out to see what all the shouting was about.

But in the police car all his aggression collapsed. Suddenly he turned to Hazel Savage, and admitted that he had murdered Heather and buried her in the garden. He told her that the police were digging in the wrong place. Later that afternoon he dictated a confession to killing his daughter, dismembering her body with a saw-edged knife he used for frozen food, and burying it in the garden. He had not intended to kill her, he said, but Heather had been sneering at him, and he decided "to take that smirk off her face" and grabbed her by the neck.

Back at Cromwell Street, a policeman told Rose West that she was being arrested for the murder of her daughter; Rose fell back on the settee, sobbing. A few minutes later she was taken away for questioning.

Stephen, Mae and Stephen's girlfriend Andrea sat in the empty house, eating crisps, drinking tea, and looking out of the window at the digging. To them it all seemed insane. They had no doubt whatever that the police were wasting their time. When the investigators found a small bone that proved to be a chicken's, Stephen and Mae ran around the kitchen, making "chook chook" noises.

The telephone rang; it was Hazel Savage, asking them to go to the police station. One of the policemen gave them a lift — the police had become much more friendly now Fred and Rose were not in the house. They were taken into the pink-painted interview room at Bearland police station.

There Fred West's solicitor Howard Ogden joined them — a fat man, with gigantic metal-rimmed spectacles, who specialised in legal aid cases, and was willing to come out at any hour of the day or night; he had represented the Wests in the rape case involving their daughter. He was accompanied by a middle-aged woman named Janet

Leach, a volunteer who had been appointed as Fred's counsellor.

Ogden lost no time in coming to the point. "I'm sorry to tell you this, but your father has admitted to killing Heather."

Stephen felt so shattered that he slid down the wall, and sat on the floor, sobbing. Andrea put her arms around him and cuddled him.

Mae refused to believe it. When Ogden said that West had confessed to strangling her, Mae declared that he had made it up. Stephen now suggested that his father was mentally ill, and needed help. They found the idea of murder impossible to face.

While they had been away, Fred West had been taken back to 25 Cromwell Street. He must have been dismayed to see that the police were now digging all over the back garden, and not simply where he had advised them to dig. He assured them that they were wasting their time extending the search, and took them to the site at the end of the garden, pointing to a spot between the wall of the Seventh Day Adventist Church next door, and a row of fir trees.

Rose was being interviewed at the Cheltenham police headquarters. She was playing it for sympathy, without the indignation and foul language. Her children, she said, had rejected her. That was why she had made no attempt to find Heather; her eldest child had "cut her off."

The police had a surprise for her. They told her that her husband had confessed to murdering Heather. Rose looked shocked.

"So she's dead? Is that right?"

They confirmed it, and told her that they believed she was involved. She shouted indignantly: "It's a lie", and began to sob.

When the interview was resumed the detectives told her bluntly that they believed it was impossible for her not to know that her daughter was buried in her garden. But she had already prepared her first line of defence. Fred often sent her off to sleep with clients, and told her not to come back until some early hour of the morning. Perhaps, she suggested, that was when he buried Heather.

Asked how she felt about all this, she replied: "Well, I feel a bit of a cunt."

"And how do you feel about him now?"

"If I ever get my hands on him", said Rose aggressively, "he's a dead man."

That night, alone in the house, Stephen and Mae found it hard to sleep. The next morning, Saturday, the digging began early. But in spite of West's precise instructions, they were still unable to locate Heather. Stephen and Mae watched them from the kitchen window. But their disbelief was slowly leaking away. A friendly policeman told them that their father had declared that when the digging reached a certain depth there would be a stream running across the garden. How, Stephen wondered, could he know this unless he had dug there?

By four o'clock it was getting dark, and it was raining steadily, so the police were wearing yellow waterproofs. Only one small piece of bone had been found, but it was stained brown, and the pathologist, Professor Bernard Knight, of Cardiff Royal Infirmary, thought it might easily have been some ancient bone from the days when Gloucester was a Roman fort.

Then, just as it began to seem that this was another wasted day, a sickening smell of decaying flesh suddenly told them that they had found what they were looking for.

2
BODIES

Professor Knight was lucky; he had no sense of smell. As the other diggers staggered back and tried not to vomit, Knight stooped by the two foot hole, and brought out a mud-covered object that looked like a bone. Washing under a tap revealed that it was indeed a femur — a human thighbone. He plunged his hands into the squelchy mess at the bottom of the hole, and began to take out bones.

Back in the house, Stephen and Mae were unaware of what was happening — the crowd of photographers outside made them keep the curtains closed — until the friendly policeman, Bob, came in and told them that they had found Heather's body. He explained that it had taken so long because they had dug crosswise. Stephen said later: "It was the worst time of my life. I had convinced myself that they would not find anything."

As they peered out of the window the strong wind suddenly blew up the tarpaulin, and they were able to see a pile of clay, and bones piled beside the hole. Mae felt sick and turned away.

By the time Knight had finished he had also found fragments of a black bin liner, and two pieces of rope. Ominously, there were also fingernails which looked as if they had been pulled out.

The bones were taken to Gloucester police station, where Knight washed them, and settled down to the task of sorting them out like a jigsaw puzzle. Heather had been decapitated and chopped into pieces.

Oddly enough, certain bones seemed to be missing — no less than twenty-two finger and toe bones (out of a total of seventy-six), as well as one kneecap. It looked in fact as if her killer had severed her fingers and toes.

And now the skeleton lay on the table, practically complete, Knight noticed something that shocked him. He had a femur — a thigh bone — left over. It was not old enough to be a Roman remain. This meant that there had to be another body in the garden.

When Rose — in the same building — was told that there might be more than one victim, she exclaimed "Oh, this is too much!" as if her patience was being sorely tried.

At the Bearland police station Fred was describing how he had killed Heather, having been intolerably provoked by her smirk. He had seized her by the throat, "and the next thing, she's gone blue ... I put her on the floor, blowed air into her mouth ... and pumped on her chest." So he cut off her legs with an ice saw, then her head, and put her in a dustbin, which he rolled down the garden, and left covered up.

Rose, he said, was out during this time.

Later, he dismembered the body in the bathroom, and buried it at the bottom of the garden. It happened at night, when he had "sent Rose away" (a euphemism for sending her off to sleep with a client).

At about this point, police came in and told him that they suspected there was another body buried in the garden.

It must have been an unpleasant moment for Fred West. His original confession — in the police car — had obviously been made because he realised that the police were going to unearth a body. But they had no reason to suspect that he had killed more than one person. So when they found Heather, they would probably stop digging. This is why he had offered to go and show them exactly where to dig, and why, when he found them digging outside the bathroom, he told them they were wasting their time, and led them to the bottom of the garden. With luck, he would escape with a manslaughter charge, while Rose would go free ...

Now they realised there was more than one body, all his hopes collapsed.

It must have required some quick thinking. They were going to find the second body anyway. So if he now made what appeared to be a full confession, there might still be time to prevent them from looking beyond the garden.

And at that point Fred decided to admit that there were two more bodies buried in the garden. One was a lodger called Shirley Ann Robinson, who was pregnant by Fred — even though she was a lesbian. He was not sure of the name of the other victim, referring to her simply as "Shirley's mate." She was buried by the bathroom wall — the spot that he had tried to direct the police away from.

The police now questioned him about the rape of a 17-year-old girl called Caroline Raine, which had occurred in December 1972 — they had found a faded press cutting about it at 25 Cromwell Street. Apparently Fred and Rose West had appeared in Gloucester Magistrate's Court on January 12, 1973, both charged with indecent assault and causing actual bodily harm. It seemed that they had seen

Caroline in Tewkesbury on the afternoon of Wednesday, December 6, 1972, and offered her a lift to her home in Cinderford. Caroline had been their nanny and au pair for six weeks in the previous October, but had left because of Fred's sexy innuendos and Rose's habit of bursting into the bathroom when she was naked. Now, because she knew them, she accepted their offer of a lift without hesitation. But instead of taking her home West had punched her unconscious, bound her with tape, and taken her back to Cromwell Street, where she was stripped. Rose West then performed oral sex on her — a sexual variation with which the 17-year-old was unacquainted — and she had been lashed with a belt. When she had agreed to keep silent about the assault, and to return to Cromwell Street as their nanny, they let her go. But her mother had noticed her bruises, and the missing skin where the adhesive tape had been torn off. Caroline had finally told her mother what happened, and she had called the police.

When the Wests agreed to plead guilty, Caroline's presence in court had not been necessary, and she had decided not to go. The result was that a lenient magistrate gave the Wests the benefit of the doubt, and fined them a total of £100.

Now, twenty-one years later, the police wanted to know about Rose's co-operation in the assault, since it obviously raised the possibility that she had been involved in the murder of the women in the garden. But here Fred dug in his heels, and insisted that the blame was entirely his own. "I was trying to get her on lesbian, and see how she reacted." In other words, he wanted to see whether Rose would enjoy sex with a woman. But, according to West, Rose had backed out. He had wanted to take Caroline home and indulge in a little bondage sex. But when Rose had touched her she had screamed, and "that was Rose finished." Instead Rose had talked to her sympathetically, made her tea, then breakfast, and finally let her go. To judge by Fred's version, it was hard to see what Caroline had to complain about ...

Quite clearly, Fred West was determined to protect his wife, whatever happened.

The next day, Sunday, was frustrating for everyone. Although Fred had shown them where to look for the other bodies, the police were unable to find them. Rose was told she was under arrest for two other murders, and questioned at length; but she continued to insist that she knew nothing. Fred was charged with the murder of Heather that evening. Finally, Rose was released on police bail, and returned to Cromwell Street.

The first thing she told the children was that they were only spending one more night in the house, then leaving. That night, they all slept in the same room, with Stephen and Andrea in the double bed, and Mae and Rose on mattresses.

The next day was equally depressing. They were taken to a "safe house" at nearby Longlevens, where they would be hidden from the press and sightseers. There was very little furniture, and no curtains. All were in a state of tension, and when Mae's cat walked over Stephen's puzzle he hit the cat, and Mae hit Stephen. Stephen's response was to hit Mae hard enough to knock her unconscious. Rose flew into a rage, and rang the police, telling them that she was not going to stay with Stephen if he was going to behave like his father. Stephen apologised, but the episode left behind some bad feeling.

Back in the garden at Cromwell Street it was continuing to rain hard, and there was still no sign of another body. Finally, at 5.20, the team digging by the wall of the bathroom which had once been a garage smelt the now familiar stench of rotting flesh, indicating that they had found "Shirley's mate" — in fact, a schoolgirl named Alison Chambers, who had vanished in 1979. Once again, the body had been dismembered and decapitated. A purple belt that passed under the chin and around the top of the skull indicated how the victim had been prevented from screaming. Knight's examination revealed that once again there were missing bones, such as kneecaps, and some fingers and toes. Already it was beginning to emerge that Fred West had some curious sexual perversion connected with fingers and toes. The possibilities were so horrible that no one chose to speculate what it might be.

The digging went on, and at about nine o'clock the searchers found the remains of Shirley Ann Robinson. It had been a long and hard day, and they decided to go home, and leave further exploration until the next morning. As usual, the worst job went to the policeman who had to sit over the grave until dawn.

The following morning, Knight looked at the remains of Shirley Ann Robinson. There was still some recognisable flesh in the grave, including brain tissue. The head, as usual, had been removed, and the body hacked up — apparently with particular force, suggesting that Fred West had been venting his anger as he dismembered her. The remains of a seven-month foetus were found close to the body, but separate from it. Fred West was later to claim that he had cut the baby from her womb in an effort to keep it alive, but missing fingers and toes suggested that he was trying to cover up his strange obsession with dismemberment.

Now at last it was clear to Detective Superintendent John Bennett — who had been placed in charge of the operation — that there might be many more bodies buried at 25 Cromwell Street, and he announced that the search would continue inside the house. The furniture was removed, and police moved in. But not before the *Daily Mirror* had somehow succeeded in getting into the house with a photographer. The result was a headline: SO NORMAL, SO CHILLING, and a subheading: "Exclusive: Inside the House of Horror." The front-page photograph showed the kitchen where Stephen, Andrea and Mae had sat watching the digging, with its formica table, and the French windows that led out into the garden. "Police fear that as many as twenty people could have been buried beneath it." The inside photographs showed the Wests' sitting-room, the first-floor bar with its inverted bottles on the optic, the "secret bedroom" on the top floor with its four-poster bed, the Wests' bedroom, with a lace canopy over the bed, the bathroom, and the children's bedroom in the cellar, with a cuddly toy owl on the pillow of the bed.

This was probably the last picture of the house as it had been. That day the police began moving out the furniture, and searching for any sign of a spot where a body might be buried — for example, below the floorboards.

By the following morning — Wednesday — the story exploded on to the front pages. Most British newspapers had pictures of the back garden of 25 Cromwell Street — looking, as one policeman remarked, "like the Somme" — with a red mechanical digger, and half a dozen men with shovels dressed in yellow oilskins. Soon journalists from all over the world were pouring into Gloucester — German, French and Brazilian TV crews were the first to arrive. Japan seemed particularly interested in the "House of Horrors", and a representative of TVS Tokyo explained that there had been a few serial killer, in Japan, but the last had been twenty years ago.

Understandably, the inhabitants of Gloucester were not averse to catering to the needs of the visitors, for their town had no tourist trade. An ice cream van and a hamburger stall moved to Cromwell Street, and a local named Sean began selling T-shirts bearing the inscription: "Nightmare on Cromwell Street." People who owned houses with a view of number 25 allowed paparazzi into their homes to take photographs at £5 a time. A Pakistani whose house overlooked the back garden was able to charge photographers £50 a time, and television crews twice that. Locals even charged journalists a pound to use their lavatories.

There were the inevitable comparisons with other "houses of horror" — 10 Rillington Place, where Reginald Christie had murdered six women in the 1940s and 1950s; 16 Wardle Brook Avenue, where the Moors Murderers Ian Brady and Myra Hindley killed four children; 23 Cranley Gardens, the home of homosexual killer Dennis Nilsen, who killed 15 young men; and even 39 Hilldrop Crescent, where the "mild murderer" Crippen had dismembered his wife in 1910. The *Daily Telegraph* ran a story about nine unsolved murders of women that had taken place over the past thirty months, while the *Daily Mirror* claimed that "experts" had revealed that there were four serial killers on the loose in Britain at this moment. Further down the same page, a headline "Spare my Garden" introduced a story claiming that Fred West had begged police to put everything back exactly where they had found it. "I do not want my garden ruined." Incredibly, this story was true. West had been upset when he came back to show the police the site of the graves, and saw the state of his garden. At that stage he had no doubt that the family would continue to live at 25 Cromwell Street, and that when he had served ten years for murder — with a three-year remission for good conduct — he would be rejoining them there.

On March 2, the day Professor Knight removed Shirley Robinson's bones from her grave, the *Daily Express* devoted the bottom half of its front page to the "Garden of Death", and the top half to photographs of Princess Diana and Major James Hewett, who had just revealed that he had been her lover. It would be the last day for some time that the House of Horror would have to share top billing with anyone else.

Even at this early date, *Today* had done its homework, and produced a brief but — on the whole — surprisingly accurate piece that contains some interesting nuggets of information. Under the headline: "Dad Doted On His Ten Kids", it reported:

"To the outside world, Frederick West was a loving father who headed a huge family of ten children. He married his childhood sweetheart Catherine Costello when he was 21, and they had two daughters.

"That marriage failed, but when it split up, it was West who took the girls, Anna, now 30, and Charmaine, to live with them as he moved around looking for building work.

"In 1972 he married his second wife Rosemary Letts. They had six children: Mae, 21, Stephen, 20, Leanne, Louise, Barry, 13, plus Heather. Rosemary also had two girls, Roxy and Luciana, from a previous relationship.

"Yesterday, West's younger brother Doug, 47, said: "Fred was such a gentle guy — he wouldn't hurt a fly."

"He was often bullied at school, and our other brother John would have to stick up for him.

"He was a superb dad. His work and his family were the two great loves in his life.

"He loved those kids and he would give you his last shilling if you needed it."

Retired Joe Hefferan, 67, was a neighbour in Cromwell Street for 22 years.

"They were a lovely family. I used to say hello to the children as they were coming and going from the house to school.

"I knew Heather, and I was shocked when I heard what had happened.

"I used to see Fred working all hours. He never went to the pub. He just worked and spent time with his family."

A young mother who lived further down the road, and did not want to be named, said one of her daughters had been to the Wests' house to play.

"She used to come home and tell me about playing in the cellar with a trapdoor covered by a carpet."

"Another neighbour said: "They were a quiet family who kept themselves to themselves. You couldn't just go and knock on their door.

"They had an extra set of gates put up with a bell on, so if you went through them they always looked through the window.

"This was just a typical inner-city street, but you never know what goes on behind closed doors."

This then was the picture that West presented not only to the world but to his siblings: a loving father, a "gentle guy who wouldn't hurt a fly", a man who was obsessed by his work and his family.

West's brother Doug also described in another interview how West would play with his children on the floor, giving them piggy backs.

But the tone of the reports soon began to change. A few days later, under the headline: "Home which never rang with laughter", the *Mail* printed an interview with Rose's mother Daisy, explaining that Rose had been just 15 when she met Fred West in the village of Bishop's Cleeve, and that her parents were horrified, because Rose had never had a boyfriend before. They contacted the social services and had Rose taken into care. But this only lasted for three weeks, until her 16th birthay, when she had to be released. She then moved into a caravan with Fred West and his two children.

"Maybe it was our fault", said Daisy, "We were so strict with our children, and sex was never discussed. Maybe she ran off with him as a rebellion against her upbringing."

The *Mail* article explained that "Rosemary had enjoyed a happy but disciplined childhood. Both her father William, an electrical engineer, and Daisy were strict with their seven children. Although beatings were rare, a few parental sharp words generally ensured obedience and impeccable manners. Graham Letts, 37, a painter and decorator — who together with his wife Barbara had been one of the most frequent visitors at 25 Cromwell Street — recalls: "Mum and dad played very heavily on psychological punishment ... It was very much the "Wait until your father gets home regime."

Rose, he explained, was the prettiest of the girls, and despite parental strictness never lost her spirit. But the girls never dared bring a boyfriend home. "Sex was taboo."

"West's family grew rapidly with the birth of

Stephen and Mae, and then more children arrived, Tara, Louise, Barry, Rosemary and Lucyanna. Tara, Louise and Lucyanna were obviously of mixed blood.

Although to the outside world Fred and Rose were dedicated parents, the atmosphere inside Cromwell street was "eerie", said Graham. There was no laughter from the children. They were always immaculately turned out. Their manners were impeccable. But they were so subdued it was unnatural.

"Whenever we walked into the house, there was never any noise. Even with nine or ten children around, you could hear a pin drop. Barbara and I felt that it was probably because Rosie was so strict with them. If the children looked like playing up, just a half-glance from Rosie was enough. There was no shouting or screaming. It reminded me in some ways of our mum and dad when we were kids. Rosie was every bit as strict, and seemed to be using the same tactics. Nothing was stated, but the message was clear: if you don't do as I say, you'll regret it.

"Rosie and Fred were always fine with us, though. Sometimes when we called, Fred would sit quietly in a corner, which was his way of saying he'd rather we weren't there."

What seemed to be emerging very clearly is that Fred was regarded as the quiet and placid one, while Rose was the stern disciplinarian.

It was Friday, March 4, three days after the police had moved their equipment inside 25 Cromwell Street, and still no more bodies had been found. The investigation seemed to be at a standstill. Fred West was being questioned in sixteen-hour sessions, but was still stonewalling. The police had learned that his wife Rena and her baby Charmaine had not been seen since the early 1970s, but West would not admit to killing them.

Then, at 5.35 on Friday afternoon, he scrawled a note which said: "I, Frederick West, authorise my solicitor Howard Ogden to advise Supt Bennett that I wish to admit a further (approx) 9 killings, expressly Charmaine, Rena, Lynda Gough and others to be identified. F.West."

The "approx" was typical. He did not even seem certain how many bodies were buried at Cromwell Street, and was certainly not sure who they were. But that evening he agreed to show the police where to look, and proceeded to draw a plan of the cellar. There was also, he said, a girl buried under the bathroom floor.

That same afternoon, an electronic probe had been brought into 25 Cromwell Street: it had been developed for finding mines — and bodies — in the Falklands war. Now it was used in the bathroom, and seemed to indicate something buried under the floor. After that it was taken to the cellar. Fred West, disguised as a policeman, was taken along to the house — he had agreed to co-operate when the police told him that they would be forced to knock the whole house apart unless he pointed out the bodies. He seemed upset to find the house devoid of furniture. But he used a can of spray paint to draw on the cellar floor the spots where he recollected burying the bodies — six of them, he thought. In fact the radar device could only find five spots where the ground had been disturbed — West had lost count of the corpses he had buried.

The next morning — Saturday — the first of the bodies in the cellar was unearthed. Again it had been decapitated and dismembered. It was behind a false chimney breast, which may have been an attempt at concealment, or simply an addition to the children's bedroom. A piece of cloth knotted into a circle seemed to have human hair trapped inside it, and looked as if it had been used — like the belt around the earlier skull — to keep the mouth closed.

While this was happening, West had been taken by the police to a field between Kempley and his childhood home Much Marcle, not far from where he had lived in a caravan with his wife Rena; he showed them the spot where he thought he had buried Rena's body.

The next body, found near the opposite wall, close to a fireplace decorated with pictures of Marilyn Monroe, had a mask of tape wrapped round the face, and a plastic tube — obviously so the victim could breathe — sticking out of one nostril.

The next morning another body was found, the sixth so far. The skull again had cloth wrapped round it. A sharp knife was found among the bones.

The seventh body was unearthed on Sunday morning — like the others, decapitated and dismembered. A length of plastic-covered clothesline was also found in the grave. The victim had been gagged with a bra, tights and two pairs of nylon socks, and a pair of nylon knickers was found in the grave. Death was apparently due to a blow on the back of the head with a ball-headed hammer.

The eighth body — the one West had already admitted was under the bathroom floor — was found on Monday evening; West had told them that her name was Lynda Gough. The bathroom had originally been a garage, and West had buried her in what had been the inspection pit. The fact that this body was also decapitated and dismembered — when there would have been plenty of room to bury it intact — seemed to indicate that West had been lying when he told police that he dismembered his victims to save space. It became increasingly obvious that

West had some peculiar perversion associated with dissection and dismemberment. And again, as in the case of all the other corpses, there were missing fingers and toes. West always refused to discuss the missing bones.

It was the following evening, Tuesday, that the ninth body was found beneath the cellar floor. Again she had been decapitated and dismembered. Water seepage had hastened decomposition — the high water table in the area had already complicated digging in the garden.

On the day the ninth body was discovered, 25 Cromwell Street had to be shored up with concrete to prevent risk of collapse.

As the bodies were unearthed, the press went into a kind of feeding frenzy. There had been nothing quite like this since those days in the spring of 1953 when body after body had been found at 10 Rillington Place, the residence of the sex murderer Reginald Christie. But Christie had at least left the female corpses intact, not hacked them into fragments. The masking tape around the faces of West's victims also revealed evidence of some kind of sexual torture.

One journalist had enough patience to count the crowd outside 25 Cromwell Street; there were 75 journalists and cameramen, and three hundred sightseers.

The first revelations about Fred and Rose West seemed puzzling. A forklift truck driver revealed how when he was 17 (in 1977), he had met Rose in a night club, walked her home, and had sex against the wall. Rose was 24 at the time, and her husband 36. Was Fred West so inadequate in bed that his wife needed casual sex encounters?

The answer appeared a few days later in the *Sun*, in a headline: FOUR MEN A NIGHT, with a subheading: "Sex-crazed Rose could just not get enough." The source of this information was Mae's former boyfriend. "She was a nymphomaniac — she just couldn't get enough." And he revealed how, on his first visit to the house, Rose had walked out of the bathroom naked. "Everything was sagging and dangling everwhere. It was a pretty horrible sight." Mae had gasped: "Mother!", but Rose had commented: "He'll soon get used to it."

The former boyfriend told how, when he was helping Fred to lay a carpet, and Rose was sitting on the settee with her legs apart, he glanced up to realise that she was wearing no knickers.

When he first knew Mae, he revealed, there was a "stream of black guys knocking at the door."

He described how he had met Mae in the Pint Pot pub when she was sixteen, and he was celebrating his eighteenth birthday. When he first came to the house Fred answered the door and asked aggressively: "What can I do for you, mate?"

But when he learned that the caller was Mae's boyfriend his attitude became friendlier. He was not then aware of the reason: that for more than two years Fred West had been trying to force incest on Mae, but had been frustrated by the alliance between Mae and Heather. Since her body began to fill out, Mae had changed into trousers as soon as she came home from school, because if her father caught her wearing a skirt, he lost no time in putting his hand up it — he was not embarrassed about doing this in front of the rest of the family. He often lifted her blouse, removed her bra, and fondled her breasts. And if she took a shower without Heather keeping guard, he would reach around the shower curtain and fondle her; the fact that he often went on for as long as twenty minutes suggests that he was masturbating at the same time. Now a boyfriend had appeared, Mae might cease to be so averse to sex. So he lost no time in encouraging him to stay the night in Mae's room.

In fact, the teenagers were embarrassed. Mae's experience of her father and mother, and her rape at the age of eight, had made her feel that sex was "dirty." She enjoyed kissing and cuddling, but had no wish to go further. So the boyfriend spent the night on her settee. And when Fred enquired jovially the next morning what Mae had been like in bed, he blushed and looked away.

But after four months, he moved in, and Mae lost her inhibitions about sex, and he became her lover.

Now Mae had joined the sex club, West stopped importuning her. It was probably enough to feel that she had lost her prudishness. He was willing to bide his time.

The former boyfriend went on to describe how one day, Fred put on a film he had videoed for them, and how he inserted by mistake a video that showed Rose being possessed by a black man. This may have been the same man who came regularly for sex every Sunday afternoon. He would wait patiently while Rose finished giving the children their dinner, then Rose would go upstairs to "get ready", and the black man would soon follow her. A red light would go on in the sitting-room, to show that she was not to be disturbed. But an hour later Fred would go up and join them ...

He also mentioned that Fred and Rose enjoyed driving out into the country for "sex parties", with the van loaded up with blankets and mattresses. There were, he said, other men taking part — dropping the first hint of a rumour that still persists: that there were others involved in the Wests' orgies.

The forklift driver who had admitted to having sex

with Rose against a wall, gave a long interview to the *Daily Mirror* under the headline: I MADE LOVE IN BATHROOM THAT HID A BODY. It seemed, he had subsequently become a tenant at 25 Cromwell Street, and described how his "girlfriend" (he did not specify if this was Rose, but it clearly was) had rolled back a carpet in the extension, and pulled up a trapdoor that led down to the cellar. There were six or seven mattresses on the floor, and they began making love at one end, and worked their way through them. His "girlfriend", he said, would "scream and yell" as they made love — a habit for which Rose was well known among tenants of the house. (One described how she used to turn up the radio to drown Rose's shrieks of joy.)

The man mentions making love with a second girl in the cellar — again without mentioning her identity. But by this time Anne Marie was 13, and had been forced by Rose and Fred to prostitute herself to Rose's lovers since she was ten.

On the same page Rose's younger brother, Graham Letts, spoke of his "anguish" at having helped Fred to cover the cellar floor with a foot of concrete, sealing in five corpses.

3
SEXUAL FREE-FOR-ALL

But who were the victims in the basement? The natural assumption was that they were girls who had come to live in the house. But this soon proved to be incorrect. Four of the five basement victims would prove to be strangers to 25 Cromwell Street.

Establishing the identities proved to be an enormous task. Fred West had stated that the first body found in the basement was that of a Dutch girl, whom he referred to as "Tulip." Gloucester police contacted the police in Holland, Germany and Switzerland to enquire about missing girls. A similar enquiry about girls who had vanished in England since the 1970s brought in a flood of literally hundreds of names.

Dr David Whittaker, an oral biologist from the University of Wales College of Medicine, was given the task of comparing photographs and descriptions of the girls with what he had been able to glean from the skulls and teeth of the victims. His skill as an odontologist led to the nickname "the Tooth Fairy."

The skulls had to be photographed at exactly the same angle as the photograph of the suspected victim, after which a transparent photograph of the skull had to be superimposed on the face. It was a method that had been used by pathologist John

Glaister in 1935, when Dr Buck Ruxton of Lancaster was accused of murdering his wife and their maid, and throwing their dismembered bodies into a river. Mrs Ruxton's long, horse-like face, superimposed on the skull found in the river, left no one on the jury in any doubt that it was the same person.

The first of the unknown victims to yield her identity to this method was the ninth body found at Cromwell Street, and it became clear that she had never been one of the Wests' lodgers. Carol Anne Cooper was the product of a broken home, and had been placed in the care of social workers. In 1973, at the age of 15, she had been living in the Pines Children's Home in Worcester. On Saturday, November 10, she had been to the cinema with her boyfriend, Andrew Jones, and other friends. At 9 in the evening, he saw her to a bus stop — she was on her way to spend the rest of the weekend with her grandmother — and waved goodbye to her. This was the last he saw of her.

The police reasoned that she had been offered a lift to the children's home when she got off the bus — or forcibly dragged into a car. She had been taken back to Cromwell Street, subjected to "bondage" and rape, and finally killed. She had been the first victim to be buried in the cellar.

According to Fred West, Rose had never been present when the girls were abducted or killed. But was it likely that a lone girl would get into a car with a strange man? Recalling the abduction of Caroline Raine in December 1972, the police felt it was far more likely that Fred and Rose had cruised around together, like the Moors Murderers Ian Brady and Myra Hindley, giving their potential victims a false sense of security.

When the police went back to Caroline Raine —

whose 1972 statement had been lost — they soon realised that what had emerged in court in January 1973 had been far short of the truth.

Caroline Raine had been almost 17 when she first met Fred and Rose West, one evening in early October 1972; she was thumbing a lift from Tewkesbury — where her boyfriend lived — back home to the village of Cinderford. She was often given a lift by a friendly telephone engineer, but since it was cold and damp she was glad to accept a lift from this married couple who stopped their grey Ford Popular.

On the way there they talked, and Caroline mentioned that she was hoping to leave home — where she was one of fifteen children — to find a job. The Wests immediately offered her a job as a live-in nanny and au pair, at a wage of £3 a week. Caroline accepted promptly. The next day Fred and Rose turned up at Caroline's home with their four children, Anne Marie, Heather, baby Mae, and Steve, West's illegitimate son (who was living with them at the time — not to be confused with West's legitimate son Stephen). Caroline took an immediate liking to them. Soon after, she moved into 25 Cromwell Street — only two months after the Wests had moved in.

The Wests already had two male lodgers. Rose West had joined them for sex on the very first day they had moved in. They were equally lucky with the new nanny, who had sex with both of them in the room they shared, after an evening of drinking and music. During the six weeks she spent in the house Caroline also had sex with her boyfriend, who stayed the night, as well as an ex-boyfriend in the navy.

She had no way of knowing that giving herself to a number of men under their roof was the most certain way she could have chosen to make both Fred and

Rose West quite determined to possess her. The very idea of a woman being possessed by another man was enough to throw Fred into a frenzy of desire, while 19-year-old Rose had already a well-developed taste for lesbian intercourse. (She said she preferred it to sex with males because it was more tender.)

Fred's method of preparing Caroline for seduction was to talk endlessly about sex — particularly group sex, lesbianism, and the abortions he claimed to have performed. But what really bothered her was Rose's advances. At first, when Rose told her she had nice eyes, she simply took it as a compliment from one woman to another. But when Rose took a strand of her hair and twisted it in her fingers, then stroked it, she began to feel nervous. And when Rose began to take every opportunity of walking into the bathroom when she was in the bath, Caroline decided it was time to leave. She did so after intervening in a quarrel between Rose and Fred, taking Rose's side. She may have felt that Rose would make this an excuse for further intimacies.

Fred and Rose were not accustomed to having a prize snatched away at the last moment. In their four years together, both had become accustomed to getting what they wanted. A neighbour of their days at Midland Road, Liz Agius, would tell how, after resisting their blandishments about group sex, she had felt dizzy after drinking some tea, and awakened to find herself naked in bed with Fred and Rose — and that Fred admitted he had had sex with her while she was unconscious.

Now, according to West's later "confessions", Rose told Fred that they would have to "get" Caroline (Fred admitted that he was prepared to kill her for the sake of possessing her), and the two began planning how this could be done. They knew that when Caroline went to see her boyfriend she would hitch-hike home. On Wednesday, December 6, 1972 — just a week after Rose had turned 19 — they were waiting for her. After she had said goodnight to her boyfriend they pulled up alongside and offered her a lift. She of course had no reason to refuse. She climbed into the back of the car, and Rose West joined her, saying she wanted a "chat."

At first that was all she did — tell her how the children missed her, and ask how she was getting on. Then, as they drove towards Gloucester, Fred raised the subject that was foremost in his mind — whether she had had sex with her boyfriend — the very thought was obviously enough to make him flush with desire. Caroline was embarrassed and said no.

By now Rose was making advances, stroking her hair, touching her legs, and trying to kiss her on the mouth. When Rose began feeling her breasts, and Fred asked "What's her tits like?" Caroline began to resist actively, telling her to "Get off." At this point Fred pulled in to the side of the road, by a five-barred gate. Then he turned round, told Caroline she was a bitch, and punched her in the face until she lost consciousness.

When she came to, a few moments later, her hands were tied behind her back with her own scarf, and Fred was binding tape round her mouth. Rose then pushed her down on to the seat and sat on her. She was panic-stricken, and had to breathe through her nose. Now able to allow her hands to roam at will, Rose continued to fondle her.

Street lights made Caroline aware they were back in Gloucester. They parked in front of 25 Cromwell Street, and as Fred dragged her out of the car he was laughing and feeling under her clothes. It was about midnight, and Cromwell Street was quiet.

She was taken up to the first-floor bedroom, where there was a settee and a mattress. There Fred told her that he would remove the tape if she was a good girl, and cut the tape off her face, apologising for a small cut he made on her ear. The sticky tape pulled out some of her hair.

They all sat on the settee, and Rose went on trying to kiss her, and touching her breasts. Finally, Rose went out and made tea. The three of them sat and drank it.

The Wests now removed all her clothes except her shoes — they must have found it sexually stimulating to leave these on — then her hands were tied behind her. She was gagged with cotton wool, and laid on her back on the bed. Rose then got undressed, and Caroline felt Rose's fingers entering her vagina — she was sure they were Rose's because they had long nails. Then Fred's fingers probed her. She heard him say that she was "big inside", but that her vaginal lips were too fat. "They will get in the way of the clitoris."

Now the sex began — but it was not normal sex. While Rose held her legs apart, Fred beat her genitals with a belt, using the buckle end; there were six or more strokes. After that Rose knelt down and performed oral sex — which Caroline had not only not encountered before, but had not even heard of. While this was going on Fred had undressed, and was fondling his wife's breasts and having sex with her from behind.

When this was over the gag was removed, and she was untied. While Rose went to the bathroom, Fred hastily raped Caroline, obviously anxious that Rose should not find out. After that he dressed and asked her not to tell. She noticed that he had tears in his eyes.

It was early in the morning, and the three of them

now slept. Some time during the night, Caroline crept to the window to try and escape, but since she was still tied and gagged, it was impossible to raise it.

At about seven they were awakened by a ringing at the doorbell. Fred went down, and Caroline heard some male visitor in the next room. She tried making noises, but Rose placed a pillow over her head. Fred was furious when he came back in, and told her that he would keep her prisoner in the cellar, where his black friends could have her, and then bury her under the paving stones of Gloucester. He added that there were already "hundreds of girls" there.

When Rose went out to give the children breakfast he raped her again. Then he apologised, and told her that it had all been "her idea." Once again he was crying. He begged her to come back and work for them, and since she saw that this was her only chance of escape, she agreed.

After breakfast Caroline helped clean the house, hoovering just as she used to. She played with the children, and talked briefly to the two lodgers. Fred persuaded her to take three baths in an attempt to remove the traces of sticky tape from her face and hair.

She spent most of the morning with the Wests, who now accepted that she was going home to collect her clothes, then return to Cromwell Street. Finally, Fred West dropped off the two women at a laundrette while he went to find a parking space. Caroline saw her chance; after a few minutes she remarked casually that she was going, and walked out.

Near the outskirts of Gloucester she was given a lift by the brother of a friend, and went to his home, where she described to her friend, Doreen Bradley, how she had been attacked. Then she was taken home. But she did not tell her story to her friend's brother, being too ashamed.

At home she went to bed and hid under the covers. When she came down her mother noticed the state of her face, and questioned her. Recalling West's threats to kill her if she revealed what had happened, she was at first evasive. But eventually she told her mother what had happened. Her mother insisted that she should report it, and she rang the police. A woman police constable came to see her, and as a result a young police constable called at 25 Cromwell Street the same day.

Rose was belligerent; when he told her of Caroline's accusation, she said: "Don't be fucking daft, what do you think I am?" The constable said he would like to examine the car, and Rose said: "Please your bloody self." There he found a button from Caroline's coat. In the lounge there was a roll of brown adhesive tape — such as would later be used on some of the victims. A search of the house also revealed a great deal of pornography.

Rose and Fred West were placed under arrest. Rose admitted the lesbian assault on Caroline, but Fred denied rape. Rose also insisted that when Caroline asked her to stop fondling her, she had stopped. She also made much of giving Caroline a cup of tea and comforting her.

Caroline Raine had been badly shaken by the events of that night; she said later that it had made her feel degraded and worthless, and undermined her respect for herself. So she decided to avoid the ordeal of a court appearance. (Since the Wests were pleading guilty, her evidence was not necessary.) No doubt she also had no desire to be publicly labelled a rape victim.

So when the case came to court on Friday, January

12, 1973, Caroline was not there to give evidence. Fred was charged with indecent assault and causing actual bodily harm, but not with rape. Rose faced the same charges. The defence made the most of the fact that Caroline had not screamed when her mouth was unbound, and that she had not tried to escape during the following morning, although she could have walked out at any time. The defence claimed that she had offered "passive co-operation", and made it sound as if the whole episode was a kind of joke that went wrong. It was also pointed out that the Wests had children, and the magistrates were told (untruthfully, as it happened) that Rose was seeking psychiatric help for her lesbian tendencies. It was also mentioned that she was pregnant (Stephen was to be born in August).

West did his best to look sheepish, and to give the impression of being a decent and guileless countryman; he told the magistrates: "I don't know why I did it — it just happened." And since his criminal record involved no previous sexual offences — only theft — he was believed.

The chairman of the bench, John Smith, was later to say that he felt Fred West to be an amiable and docile character, and that this had influenced his decision to fine them £50 each.

What happened to Caroline Raine is probably basically what happened to the other victims, except that Fred and Rose were now determined not to make the same mistake twice. That, of course, meant killing any future victims. And that in turn may have increased Fred's sadism. We have seen in the Introduction how Donald "Pee Wee" Gaskins was startled by his own upsurge of sadism and violence the first time he decided in advance to kill his rape victim. He told Wilton Earle: "All I could think

about was that I could do anything I wanted to her."
Gaskins tortured her with a knife before sodomising
her and then killing her. By deciding that she was a
"throwaway", he was giving rein to his darkest
impulses. The same is undoubtedly true of Fred
West.

Soon after the Wests had moved into Cromwell
Street the previous September, their first lodger, an
18-year-old, had moved into a room on the top floor,
which he shared with his friend. Soon after, he met a
girl called Lynda Gough in a Gloucester cafe; she was
a few months his senior, being 19.

Lynda Carole Gough was the daughter of a
fireman, and had been educated at a private school
for children with learning difficulties. After leaving
school she had gone to work as a seamstress at the
Co-op. But since the age of 17 she had been a
rebellious adolescent, impatient of parental restraints. Her father disliked the boy she was going
out with, regarding him as scruffy and unsuitable.
Lynda reacted badly to this attempt to dictate her life.
Her method of expressing this revolt was sexual
promiscuity. She was also, according to Fred West,
"into black magic magazines."

Now she went back to the 18-year-old lodger's
room, and was soon having regular sex with him.
When this affair ended she moved on to his friend.
Subsequently she had sex with other male lodgers.

This behaviour, of course, was enough to arouse
Fred's desire to join in. Lynda, who was reasonably
pretty and had a good figure, was also attractive to
Rose. Just as with Caroline Raine, the Wests asked
Lynda to baby-sit for them and help look after the
children. She became friendly with the Wests — and
on March 5, 1973, two people came to her home and
took her out for a drink; the woman was short, dark-

haired and plump (Rose was at this time pregnant with Stephen).

Lynda had already signalled her intention of leaving home and finding herself a flat, and on April 19 she carried it out, leaving her parents a note that said: "Dear Mum and Dad, Please don't worry about me. I have got a flat and will come and see you some time. Love Lin."

According to Geoffrey Wansell's *An Evil Love*, Lynda soon became Rose West's friend and confidante. "Rose was knocking off Lynda before I was," West is said to have claimed.

West also claimed — and Wansell seems to believe him — that Lynda was at first a willing participant in "kinky sex", and allowed herself to be hung upside down over a hole West had made in the cellar floor. But at some point West's own desire for "kinky sex" took over. And then, according to Wansell, she was abused with a vibrator and a dildo. "Other people may have been present," says Wansell, repeating a suggestion that has been made many times — that friends of the Wests (and possibly Rose's father Bill Letts) took part in the early stages of the sexual abuse. "In the hours, even days, before her eventual death Lynda Gough was reduced to nothing more than a slab of meat. Her fingers and toes were certainly cut off while she was conscious, as were her hands and wrists. Both her kneecaps were removed, as were seven ribs and her breastbone. She could not speak, she could not protest; she was utterly helpless."

Yet it must be stated that this is largely speculation — Wansell admits that West never confessed exactly what happened to Lynda and the other victims. In which case it is difficult to see how he can state so positively that "her fingers and toes were certainly cut off while she was conscious." The truth is that it is impossible to be certain of anything of the sort.

There is in fact one piece of evidence that suggests that Wansell could be wrong. When West murdered his first victim, Ann McFall, in 1967 he dismembered her body, cutting off the fingers and toes. But there is simply no reason to believe that West tortured her; he claimed that she was the only woman he had ever loved, and may well have killed her accidentally in the course of bondage-sex. So the dismemberment of Ann McFall only indicates what will slowly become clear as we consider later murders — that West was obsessed by butchery and dismemberment.

We simply do not know whether West removed his victims' fingers and toes before or after death — he never made any statement about it, and so Wansell's account must be regarded as guesswork rather than fact.

All we can say for certain is that when Lynda Gough was dead — strangled or suffocated — West would have settled down to the task of dismembering her with enthusiasm. We can say this because in the case of Lynda dismemberment was unnecessary, since he intended burying her in the inspection pit in the garage — which, even if not long enough for a full-length body, was certainly long enough for a body that had been doubled up. All the evidence indicates that West derived sexual pleasure from treating human bodies like animal carcases, and hacking them to pieces.

Lynda's parents decided not to try and find her, but to wait until she paid them a visit. But as one week dragged into two, her mother June became increasingly worried. On Saturday, May 5, 1973, she began making enquiries among Lynda's friends, and at her place of work. Finally Mrs Gough knocked on the door of 25 Cromwell Street. It was opened by the woman who had called at her home four weeks ago — two weeks before Lynda's disappearance — to take Lynda for a drink. Rose West explained that Lynda had gone to Weston-super-Mare, and her husband confirmed this. But Mrs Gough noticed that Rose West was wearing her daughter's slippers, and that some of Lynda's clothes were hanging on the washing-line in the garden. Rose West explained this by saying that Lynda had left some clothes behind. They went on to explain that Lynda had left after a quarrel about hitting Anne Marie when she was baby-sitting.

The Goughs continued to look for their daughter, reporting her missing to the police and the Salvation Army; they even went to Weston-super-Mare to look for her, and called at the labour exchange.

They had, of course, no reason to suspect the Wests of having anything to do with their daughter's disappearance — they were an apparently normal married couple with a houseful of children, and would have no reason to do harm to anyone.

That summer of 1973 the Wests began the sexual abuse of Fred's daughter, Anne Marie. In her book *Out of the Shadows*, Anne Marie gives the date as 1972, the previous year, while in *Fred and Rose*, Howard Sounes gives the date as the summer of 1972. But at her first interrogation at 25 Cromwell Street, on February 24, 1994, Rose West states that they moved into the house "about three months" after Mae's birth, which had occurred on June 1, 1972; this suggests that they moved into Cromwell Street in late August or early September.

There is another reason for believing that the sexual abuse of Anne Marie began in 1973. Anne Marie states that her father first raped her soon after her ninth birthday, which was on July 6, 1973. It is unlikely that Fred West waited a full year after first sexually abusing his daughter and beginning to have sexual intercourse with her.

Anne Marie described how, as a child she adored her father, and often told him she was going to marry him. "I was his baby and he was my wonderful, handsome dad." Her father — and step-mother — preferred her to Charmaine, because she was more docile. Anne Marie explains that "Charmaine hated Rose and told her so."

She adds: "It was obvious from the word go that Rose had a hell of a temper and was not able to control it." They were made to do the household chores, and "if you did it wrong, you got a hiding." Fred, she said, was good-tempered on the whole, but he allowed Rose to beat the children, only commenting: "Make sure you hit them where it doesn't show."

She gives an example of Rose's uncontrollable temper. After breakfast one morning she ordered Charmaine and Anne Marie to wash up their plates. Charmaine took her time doing it, telling the foul-mouthed Rose: "My real mother wouldn't swear at us."

Anne Marie was obliged to wait behind Charmaine, while Charmaine played idly with the water. Finally Rose's temper snapped, and she snatched Anne Marie's plate and broke it over her head. Anne Marie had to go to the doctor's surgery for stitches in a head wound caused by a "fall."

Clearly, Rose Letts was virtually the wicked step-mother out of fairy tales. Stephen West also tells how when he had been ordered to wash the floor Rose stepped into the bowl of water he was using, and broke the bowl over his head, leaving a permanent lump.

In the years that followed, the West children were taken to the doctor's surgery so many times that it seems surprising that the Social Services made no attempt to intervene. Anne Marie states that Rose's temper became increasingly foul, and this is confirmed by Stephen and Mae. To begin with, it is clear that this was simply because she lacked self-discipline, and lashed out whenever she lost her temper.

But other episodes suggest that her outbursts had a sexual-sadistic component. Stephen tells how one morning at school he was given a message to go home immediately. When he arrived home Rose seemed "really calm." She told him to go to the bathroom and strip naked. Then Rose ordered him to lie down and put his hands around the bottom of the toilet. His hands were then tied together so he could not move. Then, very calmly, she tied his feet together.

After that she asked him what he had done wrong. He had no idea, and denied that he had done anything. Rose then began to beat him with a leather belt, with the buckle end, hitting him at the base of the spine, and kicking him in the stomach. This continued for twenty minutes, while she shouted: "What have you done wrong?" He comments: "She looked so happy, so pleased with herself."

Finally, she told him that he had stolen some magazines from her room. He swore it was not true. She went away for ten minutes, then came back, and in "a nice, sickly sweet voice", told him to go back to school. "She was so bloody cold and unfeeling."

Heather came home with a note from her teacher saying that he had confiscated some sex magazines. It was Heather who had taken them. But Rose only laughed, and said: "Don't worry, Stephen got your beating." There was no attempt to apologise to Stephen for the injustice.

Clearly, there is something odd about this episode. If she was in fact so angry that she felt the need to summon him home from school, then why did she look so calm when he came in? Why was she calm as she tied him to the foot of the toilet? Why, as she was beating and kicking him, did she look "so happy, so pleased with herself?" A woman who is angry with her son shouts furiously as she punishes him. Why did she leave the bathroom for ten minutes before she returned to tell him to go back to school? It sounds as if she beat him until she had induced a sexual orgasm, then had to go away and sink into an armchair until her energy returned. The "nice, sickly sweet voice" is also out of character; a mother who has just flogged her son for stealing magazines from her private room would be more likely to tell him grimly: "All right, go back to school and don't do it again."

Mae comments: "We were so scared of her when she was younger because she was really nasty. She'd hit one of us and then she'd want to hit us all because she was in the mood. We'd all have to hide in our rooms and wait till she calmed down. I think she just lost control." And Stephen comments perceptively: "I think she got off on hitting us."

Mae tells how, when she was eight or nine, Rose lost her temper for some reason, and came at her with a kitchen knife. Mae was dressed only in underwear, and as Rose flicked her with the knife, she kept yelling "No, mum, no, mum." By the time Rose had finished she had tiny cuts all over her rib cage.

This is not the normal anger of a bad-tempered parent, but the abnormal anger of someone who has learned to express her sexual excitement through beating and whipping.

The composer Percy Grainger, who was also a

sado-masochist, declared that he wanted to have children so he could whip them. But he added that he would explain to them that he enjoyed it. (Fortunately, he remained childless.) Rose West seems to have used her bad temper as an excuse for using the children to satisfy her sexual excitement.

In the case of Anne Marie, physical ill-treatment — including a bath in water so hot that it scalded her — culminated in a form of rape.

Anne Marie describes how when she was eight they led her down to the cellar. She felt that something strange was going on — Rose was wearing a strange "smirk" — or, as Stephen had put it, looking pleased with herself.

Anne Marie was orderd to undress; Rose became impatient at her slowness, and ripped off the thin summer dress. She was then held down on a mattress by one of them — probably Rose — as the other assembled a strange device on the floor. Then her hands were bound together with tape, and then tied with strips of sheet to some "iron object" above her head. A bowl of water was placed between her legs.

The Wests now had a naked child standing with her arms above her head, and her legs apart — the position beloved of sado-masochists.

She shouted at her father: "Why are you doing this to me?" and found his reply incomprehensible. "Shut up. It's going to help you in later life. I'm doing what all fathers have to do."

She was gagged; then a vibrator was inserted into her vagina. She looked down in terror as a red substance like frogspawn dripped into the bowl below. "It hurt so much I just wanted to die."

After what seemed a long time Fred and Rose simply left the basement. It seems fairly certain that they went into another section of the basement — it was divided into three — and had scx. After that, they went back to Anne Marie, still suspended above the bowl, and resumed where they had left off. They were still sexually excited by what they were doing. Finally, they untied her, and she was allowed to go upstairs again. She was in such pain that she could barely limp. Rose seemed to find this funny, and laughed.

Later, in the bathroom, she gave Anne Marie a sanitary towel to put inside her underwear, and told her: "Don't worry. It's a father's job." Anne Marie was later assured that she was lucky to have such loving parents.

From then on, Anne Marie was subjected to this ordeal regularly. West invented a kind of belt that would hold a vibrator inside her as she walked around the house; she had to do the housework with a buzzing sound coming from inside her. On one occasion, when Rose had been in the bedroom with her black lover, Fred West took the sperm-filled condom, led Anne Marie into a bedroom, and inserted the condom inside her vagina. Then Anne Marie had to go and watch television with the condom inside her. In her account of it, Anne Marie seems to believe that this was some kind of experiment in artificial insemination. This seems impossible. The real reason, obviously, is that Fred found the idea of his daughter watching television with a condom full of sperm inside her immensely exciting.

Anne Marie describes how on another occasion her father made a U-shaped metal bar. One lunchtime, she was made to undress by Rose, and her legs were spread apart and tied to either end of the bar. Then Rose began lashing her and swearing at her. Fred came into the cellar, and hurriedly raped his daughter

— he had to go back to work.

For most readers, all this will seem virtually incomprehensible. How could a father and mother, who struck most of their acquaintances as an ordinary married couple, derive any satisfaction from this kind of perverted sexuality?

The answer lies in the peculiar interaction between Fred and Rose West. Their relationship was an example of what criminologists call *folie à deux*, a kind of "transmitted madness." Rose was highly dominant — a member of what zoologists call "the dominant 5%." Most of the women who belong to this dominance group are highly sexed and — as the American psychologist Abraham Maslow discovered when he conducted a study in dominance in women — highly experimental in their sex lives. Maslow found that they masturbate more, have a tendency to promiscuity, and that even when they are not lesbian, have had lesbian experiences.

Rose would have found a normal marriage, to a normal husband who expected her to be faithful, deeply boring and frustrating. Instead she found herself married to a man who wanted her to sleep with other men, and who went to some trouble to make sure that she could indulge her sexual daydreams. (How Fred became this type of person is a subject we must investigate later.)

So Rose could give way to her nymphomania without any sense of guilt. Her husband had absolved her of guilt. She could smash plates over the children's heads, and Fred would smile approvingly. She could make love with the male lodgers, and his only regret was that he could not watch — but the idea excited him so much that he liked to possess her immediately afterwards. He had made a peephole in his wife's bedroom door so that he could watch her making love, and rigged up a sound system so he could listen to her gasps of ecstasy while he watched television with the children.

Where sex was concerned, she was like a spoilt child with an indulgent father; she merely had to mention what she would like, and Fred would try to get it for her. He was a nymphomaniac's daydream husband.

It was easy enough for him to procure black males for her (she preferred blacks because, she said, they were "bigger down there"). With women, it was more difficult. But, as we have seen in the case of Caroline Raine, he did his best. Rose felt she must have Caroline, and Fred, like Aladdin's genie, set out to grant her wish.

The problem was obviously that the majority of their female lodgers had no lesbian inclinations. Besides, Rose liked young, fresh-looking girls, like Caroline Raine. Even after they nearly came to disaster over Caroline, he was willing to carry on. For Rose was also Fred's sexual daydream: the schoolgirl who loved giving herself to men, the innocent who enjoyed defiling herself.

To understand the psychology of male sexual desire, we need to recognise that it is aroused by the juxtaposition of two ideas: innocence, and the surrender of innocence. They feel supremely complimented that a girl is willing to give herself. But for Fred West, it was more than a matter of girls surrendering to him; what excited him was the idea of girls surrendering to the male sex.

In his 39th Canto, Ezra Pound makes Ulysses reflect:

"When I lay in the ingle of Circe ...

Girls talked there of fucking, beasts talked there of eating,

All heavy with sleep, fucked girls and fat leopards."

Beasts, of course, do not talk of eating. And "nice girls" do not talk of fucking. But on Circe's magic island, animals speak about eating, and girls speak about fucking. What is implied is that both are somehow against the order of nature. And so the very juxtaposition "fucked girls" has a kind of shock-effect, even for those who are not particularly prudish; they are like a pornographic novel in miniature.

West's sexuality was particularly susceptible to this idea that the words "fucked" and "girls" could be juxtaposed. The very fact that it could happen made all life a kind of pornographic novel. Stephen comments: "Dad saw sex in everything. Even if he was giving you a lift he'd say he's seen someone having it in the woods or something ... Or he'd say a girl had run out at him waving her knickers in the air to try and stop him. Another time he'd say he'd picked up a hitchhiker who was "begging for it." He'd claim she'd had her skirt hitched right up while he was trying to drive. You could never get away from sex, and if he went for a walk in the park with the dogs he would see people at it on park benches. He was obsessed with sex. We used to make a joke about it with him, saying that he turned everything around to sex, and he would laugh ... "

So the thought that Caroline Raine and Lynda Gough had given themselves to several men in the house would fuel his obsession to the point of fever: nice girls, innocent-looking girls, were quite willing to give themselves. So he had every reason for wanting to help his wife satisfy her desire to possess them. He wanted to watch, to play his own part in the pornographic novel.

Unfortunately, the girls themselves were not willing to take part. But that was not a disadvantage, for the essence of sadism is that the victim should be innocent and unwilling.

This is clearly what happened with Lynda Gough. Rose desired her, and Rose finally had her way. Lynda became the victim of the rape fantasy, and died as a result. Fred and Rose West felt no conscience about her death, for it was not a real death, but a fantasy death. Fred and Rose were moulding reality to their own design. They were the masters of reality, not — like most people — its slaves.

This is why the rape of Anne Marie was the next logical step. She was a schoolgirl, a symbol of innocence, and therefore ideal for their purpose. They might have preferred to kidnap a schoolgirl from the street, but that would have been too dangerous — even though the history of Fred and Rose West shows that, after escaping the consequences of raping Caroline Raine, they felt invulnerable. So Anne Marie was ritually deflowered. It was a ceremony they enjoyed, which is why they took so long over it, and why they went back a second time. And soon after, Fred West began raping her. One more stage of the fantasy was fulfilled; his nine-year-old daughter was his mistress. This is why he could not contain himself from boasting about his sexual prowess to his workmates. They thought that his endless tales of seduction and illegitimate children were the lies of an incorrigible fantasist; but West knew otherwise. He was doing what other men only dreamed of.

4

THE MAKING OF A MONSTER

Who was Fred West?
He was born in the small Herefordshire village of Much Marcle in 1941. His father and his grandfather had been farm labourers, and Fred was expected to follow in their footsteps. Much Marcle is a typical — and very attractive — country village in the midst of farming country, with hop fields, cider orchards and rich green grass.

His father, Walter West (born 1914 in Ross-on-Wye), had started life as a wagoner's boy, then became a farm labourer near Much Marcle, a village with a population less than 700. His first marriage, to a woman twice his age, ended when she died after being stung by a bee. A few months later, in 1939, he met sixteen-year-old Daisy Hill, a maidservant, at the village fair in Much Marcle, and when they married in January 1940 Walter had become a cow-man. Daisy was three months pregnant when she married, but the child, a girl, died soon after birth. Frederick Walter Stephen West was born in a "tied cottage", Bickerton Cottage, on Monday, September 29, 1941.

Life was hard in a tiny cottage on a cow-man's wages (£6 a month), particularly when six more children arrived: John, David (who died as a baby), Daisy, Douglas, Kathleen and Gwen. Constant childbearing made Daisy put on weight until she became huge, and she wore a leather belt around her waist, with which she occasionally chastised the children.

Fred was a mother's boy, adored and spoilt by her, and his brothers later declared that he was an unaggressive child, "soft as butter", who would rather be bullied than fight back. In fact, his younger (but stronger) brother John bullied him.

He was not particularly bright at lessons, although he did well in artwork and carpentry; by the time he left school, at fourteen, he had still not learned to write properly, or to spell. He was regarded as something of a "cissy", and his companions at school made fun of him. His brother John commented that it was easy to make him cry.

Life in this rural village in a peaceful corner of England sounds idyllic, but Fred and the other children had to work hard, helping with the harvest, picking hops and strawberries, chopping wood, milking the cows. Fred even had to kill the family pig by slitting its throat — raising the question of whether butchering animals gave him a taste for mutilation and dismembering. His schoolfellows complained because he stank of pig's muck.

Fred's childhood was permeated by a heavy atmosphere of sexuality. Writers like Howard Sounes, author of *Fred and Rose*, have shown themselves understandably reticent — Sounes contents himself with the statement that Walter "indulged in one of the greatest taboos of all: having sex with children." But Mae's former-boyfriend, was more specific: "I don't think that Fred thought he was weird at all ... His dad did it, so why can't he do it?" The same interview states: "... behind the closed doors of Moorcourt Cottage, the West family indulged in the most perverted practices. Fred West said that his father abused the family. He was to claim that he also played sex games with his sisters." And Mae goes further, and states in her book that Walter sexually abused his son.

According to the former-boyfriend, Fred claimed that his father had sex with the daughters of the family, pulling a towel off one as she emerged from the bathroom and saying: "I made you ... I'm entitled to touch you" — words that West himself would echo in later years.

Fred himself claimed to have had incestuous relations with his sisters. He quotes him as saying that, "with his sisters and other young girls ... they all used to dive in the hay, and just the back end was showing. He said: "I just used to take pot luck.""

Mae says: "According to Dad, his dad Walter taught him it was a father's duty to "break in" his daughters. I don't know if it's true or not, but I do know that Dad claimed that when he was sixteen he tried it on with one of his sisters and he was charged by the police." In fact, West was nineteen when accused of getting his thirteen-year-old sister pregnant.

The same interview states: "Most sigificantly of all, it was his own mother who introduced him to sex when he was just 12 years old." And it goes on to quote a criminal psychologist, Oliver James, as saying: "In his childhood home, deviant illicit sex was the norm. His mother having sex with him was probably the biggest factor that shaped West ... The most important thing about incest is that it breaks down the boundaries between mother and son. After that, there are no rules." Right and wrong, he says, became blurred because in West's childhood unspeakable acts were part of everyday life. "I don't think that Fred thought he was weird at all — it was just part of life. His dad did it, so why can't he do it?"

Freud once remarked that any boy who has been his mother's favourite has the perfect start in life, a sense of his own superiority. West's mother, according to her other sons, thought Fred could do no wrong, and he in turn worshipped her. Her death from a heart attack when she was only 44 shattered him.

If West had intensely disliked his father, things might have been different. But he had a deep admiration for him. Walter West was a quiet, pipe-smoking countryman who seemed to know a great deal more than he said. He was also a big, physically imposing man. So he possessed the qualities necessary to become a role model for his eldest son.

West also told his son Stephen that he indulged in bestiality with animals on the farm, and explained to him that having sex with a sheep involved putting its back legs down his wellington boots.

This quiet, unaggressive mother's boy might have grown up to be a quiet, unaggressive man if it had not been for two serious head accidents. On November 28, 1958, when he was seventeen, he ran into a girl on a bicycle; the girl was unhurt, but he was knocked unconscious after hitting a wall. He remained unconscious for almost a week, and later claimed that a metal plate had to be inserted into his head. As a result of the accident, one leg became permanently shorter than the other. He had to wear a metal brace on the broken leg.

It was after this accident that his family later claimed to observe a change in his disposition. He became subject to sudden attacks of rage. His son Stephen wrote: "Uncle John said that after the accident, Dad completely changed. He'd sit in the front room, staring at the wall and he wouldn't speak to anyone and if anyone spoke to him he'd bite their head off. He was so short-tempered that he couldn't control himself, and he's been like that ever since."

Again, when he was nineteen, he was standing on the platform of a fire escape outside a youth club, and put his hand up the skirt of a girl whom he had invited outside. She gave him a push, and he fell over the rail, striking his head. He was unconscious for twenty-four hours.

Brain damage has played a significant part in the history of mass murder, particularly of sex crime — although no one claims to be able to understand the precise neural mechanism of the change.

Dr Jonathan Pinckus, a neurologist from Georgetown University in Washington DC, has described the case of a killer who had been involved in a serious car accident at the age of sixteen, in which his head had made violent contact with the roof of the car. He was unconscious for seven days. After his recovery his personality had changed completely, and he became explosive and inclined to violence. The double murder — for which he was sentenced to death — involved stabbing both victims more than a hundred times. He showed no remorse, or any other emotion, at the death sentence. A brain scan subsequently showed heavy scar tissue in the prefrontal lobes of the brain, where his head had hit the car.

The brain has the consistency of a jelly, and is easily damaged. Behind the prefrontal lobes lies an area called the limbic system, which is concerned with feeling, emotion and aggression. The prefrontal lobes seem to be the part of the brain that inhibits violent responses and strong emotions.

In *A Mind to Crime*, Anne Moir and David Jessel note that "new brain-imaging techniques called PET

scans have revealed an abnormality in the hypothalamus (of non-violent paedophiles), the area of the
brain which controls sexuality ... ", while violent
paedophiles have the same abnormality, as well as
abnormalities in the frontal lobes and in the "animal"
area of the brain, the limbic system — the "emotional
centre."

The left and right sides of our brains have different
functions. The left side deals with language, logic,
calculation. The right side deals with patterns,
shapes, structures. You might say that the left brain
is a scientist, the right brain an artist. Or that the left
brain is intellectual while the right brain is intuitive.
People with damage to the left brain become
inarticulate, but an artist with left brain damage
could still paint a good picture. People with right
brain damage may sound perfectly normal, but one
such man could not even draw a three-leafed clover
— he drew the leaves side by side.

Since the left brain also acts as the controller of the
impulses from the right, people with left brain
damage can be violent and impulsive. They easily
explode with impatience.

A small almond-shaped object called the amygdala
(or amygdaloid nucleus), housed in the limbic
system, seems to be connected with aggression and
fear. A violent, bad-tempered ape became docile
when its amygdala was removed; a sweet old lady
became aggressive and foul-mouthed when her
amygdala was stimulated electrically — and was
baffled and shocked by her own behaviour when the
current was switched off. Close to the amygdala lies
another tiny organ called the hypothalamus, which
regulates the blood sugar. S. Hucker of the Clarke
Institute discovered abnormalities of the hypothalamus in paedophiles.

The frontal lobes of the brain are in a sense its most important part — its "executive" and planmaker. There is also some evidence to suggest that they are involved in poetic experience — Wordsworth's "glory and the freshness of a dream" — that is, in our higher emotional functions. The frontal lobes seem to exert a restraining role on the impulses of the limbic system (the "emotional brain"). Sometimes, when the impulses from the limbic system become too powerful, a person experiences a sense of loss of control. A once-popular operation called prefrontal leucotomy (or lobotomy), severing the tissue between the front lobes of the brain and the midbrain, would cause the patient to become placid — but often also dull and unintelligent.

In 1848 an efficient and popular construction foreman named Phineas Gage was tamping down an explosive in Vermont when it ignited and blew an iron bar through his skull — it traversed the frontal lobes. Gage not only survived; he was able to function normally after the wound had healed. But his character had changed completely; he had become coarse, foul-mouthed, impatient, unreliable, and unable to carry out even medium-term plans. He died during an epileptic attack thirteen years later.

Moir and Jessel report the case of a helicopter pilot who was a normal, happy family man before a crash that damaged his frontal lobes, after which he embarked on a string of love affairs, became incapable of holding down a job, and became a cheat, a liar and a swindler — in spite of which he could also exercise great charm.

The case of the "burning car murderer" Alfred Rouse provides an interesting parallel. Rouse had been a choirboy at school, and developed into a sober and responsible young man. But a head accident in the First World War, and a subsequent operation on the left temporal lobe, led to a personality change. Rouse developed an obsessive interest in sex, and as a travelling salesman seduced dozens of girls. Like the helicopter pilot, he was also known as a man of considerable charm, with a talent to entertain. Eventually his complicated sex life led to a decision to "vanish." In 1930 he picked up a hitch-hiker of roughly his own size and build, knocked him unconscious, and burned him alive in his car. He was seen while fleeing from the scene, arrested, tried and hanged.

Clearly, then, damage to the frontal lobes can decrease their ability to control violent emotion. This is almost certainly what happened to Fred West. Normally quiet and good-tempered, he could be thrown into a violent rage by frustration or opposition. In effect, West became a Jekyll and Hyde — a comment actually made by Isa McNeill, a woman who shared a caravan with West and his first wife.

Moir and Jessel also report that aggression and psychosis have been observed in a high percentage of patients with epilepsy in the temporal lobe. In 1918 a prosperous Chinese businessman named Lock Ah Tam, who was known as a generous, good-tempered and charitable man, was struck on the head by a drunken sailor with a billiard cue; his character thereafter changed completely, and he became coarse, morose, boastful and unpredictable. Eight years later, in a sudden rage, he killed his wife and two daughters with a revolver. In spite of his plea that he had suffered from epilepsy ever since the blow on the head, he was sentenced to death and executed.

The source of sexual arousal also lies in the limbic system (which houses the amygdala). If West's motorcycle accident involved damage to the limbic system, then it would explain the obsessive interest in sex as well as his sudden violent rages.

Certainly the number of sex killers who have suffered head injuries is enormous. The following list deals only with some of the most prominent.

The "French Ripper" Joseph Vacher, a tramp who raped and disembowelled victims of both sexes in the mid-1890s, had attempted to shoot himself through the head, permanently damaging one eye and paralysing the right side of his face. It is not known what part of the brain he damaged, but after years in an asylum he was released and began his career of sex murder, killing eleven before he was caught and executed in 1898.

Fritz Haarmann, Hanover's "cannibal killer", suffered from concussion after a fall from parallel bars during his training period in the army in 1900; after a period in hospital he was judged mentally deficient. After the First World War, working as an unofficial police agent, he made a habit of picking up destitute youths at the railway station and taking them to his room. The murders were not apparently pre-planned; Haarmann used to be carried away by sexual frenzy, and either strangle the victims, or suffocate them by fixing his teeth in their windpipes. He cut up the bodies and sold them for meat. Haarmann was executed in 1925.

America's "Gorilla Murderer" Earle Nelson was knocked down by a street car when he was ten years old (in 1902); it caused a hole in his temple, and made him unconscious for six days, after which he suffered from pains in the head and dizziness. After several periods in an asylum he escaped and began to roam the country, committing twenty-two sex murders between February 1926 and his capture in June 1927. He was hanged in January 1928.

Albert Fish, a child-killer who was born in 1870, began to suffer from severe headaches and dizzy spells, and also developed a stutter, after a fall from a cherry tree as a child. He committed his first murder — of a homosexual — in 1910, but had been raping small boys since his mid-twenties. He mutilated and tortured to death a mentally retarded boy in 1919, and between that time and his capture in December 1934 is believed to have committed fifteen more murders of children, one of whom (Grace Budd) he cooked and ate. (He himself claimed to have committed four hundred murders.)

Raymond Fernandez was perfectly normal until a falling hatch knocked him unconscious when he was at sea in December 1945. At 31 years of age Fernandez suddenly turned into a sex maniac, contacting lonely women through advertisements in contact magazines, and seducing them — it made no difference whether they were young or old, fat or thin, beautiful or ugly; he even seduced one seriously handicapped woman. He and his mistress Martha Beck became known as the Lonely Hearts Killers after murdering a number of women for their money, and were executed in 1951.

Richard Speck, a drifter who murdered eight nurses in a Chicago hostel in July 1966, had suffered a number of head injuries as a child, but began having severe headaches and blackouts at the age of 16 after a policeman had broken up a fight by beating him on the head several times with his club. Speck died in prison in 1991.

Gary Heidnik was tried in 1988 for keeping six black women prisoner in his basement in Philadelphia and subjecting them to a four-month ordeal of rape and torture, during which he killed two of them, cooking parts of one of the corpses and feeding it to the other prisoners. Heidnik had been mentally abnormal since he fell out of a tree as a child, deforming the shape of his head so that his schoolfellows called him "football head."

Chicago serial killer John Gacy began to have blackouts at the age of 11 after being struck on the head by a swing. He raped and murdered 33 young men between 1975 and the end of 1978, burying most of the bodies in the crawl space under his house. He was executed by lethal injection in May 1994.

Randy Kraft, a computer expert of Long Beach, California, was stopped on May 14, 1983, for careless driving, and was found to have the corpse of a young man propped up beside him in the passenger seat. A search of the car and his home revealed that he was the homosexual "Freeway Killer" who had been murdering and torturing young men since 1975 and dumping their bodies on the freeways. A list found in his car indicated that he had killed 67 men. As a child, Kraft had fallen down a flight of concrete steps and been unconscious for several hours. Kraft was sentenced to death in 1989.

Henry Lee Lucas, who claimed to have killed 360, was violently beaten by his drunken mother as a child, and on one occasion was unconscious for three days after she struck him on the head with a piece of wood. Lucas and his companion Ottis Toole wandered around America, raping and murdering at random, until they were caught in 1983. It was the case of Lucas that suddenly made America aware of the emergence of the phenomenon of the serial killer, a term coined by FBI agent Robert Ressler.

Perhaps the most interesting parallel to the case of Fred West is the serial killer Bobby Jo Long, born in 1953. A motorcycle accident in the army fractured his skull, and he remained in a coma for weeks. After this, he reported, he began thinking about sex all the time. From having sex with his wife two or three times a week he went to two or three times a day, also masturbating in between. He began committing rapes after he left the army, telephoning women who had placed classified advertisements, and if he found them alone, raping them. Then, in 1983, he changed suddenly from a non-violent rapist to a sex murderer, killing nine women. After each murder he sank into a deep sleep, and when he woke up was never certain whether he had dreamed it all — he had to go out and buy a newspaper to find out. Finally, he was touched by the story of a 17-year-old girl who had been abused in childhood, and although he raped her, let her go, knowing that it would lead to his arrest.

A doctor, Otnow Lewis, examined Long and found that he had had more than one head injury — one after falling off a swing, one after being knocked down by a car. A PET scan showed that he had damage to the left temporal lobe, and an abnormality of the amygdala. She was inclined to believe that this was responsible for Long's hyperactive sex drive.

In spite of these discoveries, Long was sentenced to death.

All this seems to suggest a high level of possibility that Fred West was turned into a mass murderer by the two accidents to his head — particularly the motorcycle crash. His upbringing in Moorcourt Cottage had made him oversexed. But without the accident he would probably have merely followed in his own father's footsteps, committing incest with his daughters. The accident meant that he flew into sudden rages in which he became murderous. And from the account given by his children Anne Marie,

Mae and Stephen, it also seems clear that he became as obsessed by sex as Bobby Jo Long after his own motorcycle accident.

Their books leave no doubt that West was a man who went around in a permanent state of raging sexual desire. His brother-in-law Graham remarked that when he and his wife visited the Wests they would often break off the conversation and vanish upstairs. They made no secret of the fact that they needed sex more urgently than other people. West even told his children that he neeeded sex every night, and would often comment to Mae that he "had a good ride" last night. Like Bobby Jo Long, he probably needed to masturbate in between times — Rose West told Mae that one of the first things she did on moving into his caravan was to throw out a large box of knickers; judging by West's general record, we can assume he stole them from clotheslines.

A year after the motorcycle accident, West met a sixteen-year-old Glasgow delinquent named Catherine Costello, known as Rena.

Catherine Bernadette Costello had been born in Coatbridge, outside Glasgow, on April 14, 1944; she — like her four sisters — was the child of a broken home; their mother had left their father when they were young. Edward Costello worked in a scrap-iron yard, and on his wages brought up his five daughters and two orphaned cousins.

Rena appeared in court for theft when she had just turned eleven, and again when she was twelve. When it happened again the following year she was given two years probation, and after that she was sent to a juvenile detention centre. Mae says that Rena was mixed up with a motorcycle gang called The Skulls, who were "into drugs." One of her schoolfriends, a girl called Margaret Mackintosh, came from Ledbury, near Much Marcle, but spent much time in Scotland, where she met Rena Costello in the detention centre. Rena decided to accompany her friend back to Ledbury. It was there, in 1960, that she met Fred, who was three years her senior. Soon they were having sex — probably in fields or barns, since Fred could hardly take her back to the overcrowded cottage, and she could hardly take him back to the room in the New Inn that she shared with Margaret. But Rena seems to have felt a strong romantic attachment, since she tattooed Fred's name on her arm with a needle and Indian ink.

It was after Rena's return to Glasgow that Fred had his second head accident, falling down the fire escape at the Ledbury youth club. Howard Sounes claims that it was after this second accident that Fred's family noted the change in his disposition, the tendency to depression and sudden violent rages.

At the age of eighteen, West began working in boats in Bristol docks; on two occasions he travelled to Jamaica on a banana boat.

Sounes interviewed one of West's closest friends at the time, Brian Hill, who tells how it was in 1961 that Fred began his career of theft. The theft sounds like the typical sudden impulse of a brain-damaged man; as they were walking through a stationery shop in Ledbury, Fred was so attracted by some women's cigarette cases that he put one in his pocket. After this they went to a jewellers, where he stole a gold watch-strap. If it is true that West began his career of theft as late as 1961 — when he was almost twenty — then it seems likely that his kleptomania was also the result of the accidents.

Alerted by the shopkeepers, police picked up the two poorly dressed youths later the same day, and they were fined £4 each.

Three months later, in June 1961, West was accused of getting his thirteen-year-old sister pregnant. He had been having sex with her since the previous December — it sounds as if the girl was dazzled by the glamour of an elder brother who had just come back from sea. Questioned about incest by a social worker, West replied: "Doesn't everybody do it?"

The reaction of his family seems to have been unexpectedly disapproving — his brother Doug told a reporter that they refused to speak to him. This can have hardly been due to shock at the incest itself — in *An Evil Love*, based on West's own confessions, Geoffrey Wansell even suggests that Walter West may have committed incest with his son present, and invited him to join in — but rather to the fact that it was now public knowledge. The important thing in small country villages was not what you did, but what your neighbours knew about you.

The child was aborted, and Fred was obliged to leave home. He moved into nearby Daisy Cottage, with an uncle and aunt.

On November 9, 1961, six weeks after his twentieth birthday, the case came to court at the Hereford Assizes, but his sister declined to name the man responsible, and it collapsed.

After the incest scandal, Fred began working as a builder's labourer. His family allowed him to return to Moorcourt Cottage after a year. Soon after his return, in the summer of 1962, Rena came back from Glasgow. She was pregnant by an Asian — one source says he was a bus driver, another that he was her pimp, a Pakistani. Apparently Rena did not even tell him she was pregnant.

In November 1960, soon after her return to

Glasgow, Rena had appeared in court in Glasgow for soliciting, but had been released with a caution. A few weeks later she appeared again charged with attempted burglary, and was sent to an approved school. Released after seventeen months, she began training as a nurse, but was soon back in court, fined £2 for theft. It was when she was working as a bus conductress that she became pregnant, and decided to go south again. By this time she had dyed her dark hair blonde.

She took a job as a waitress in a cafe in Ledbury, and the affair with Fred resumed immediately. Margaret Mackintosh, as reported by Sounes, tells a curious story of how Fred tried to perform an operation to abort her in a wood near Ledbury, but they were seen, and the police were called. After this failure they decided to marry anyway. On November 17, 1962, they stood in front of the registrar at the Ledbury Registry Office and became man and wife.

Why did Fred West decide to marry? The question may sound absurd; after all, why do most people decide to marry? Rena obviously wanted a husband because she was pregnant and rootless. But West had no reason to want a wife. He wanted every woman in the world. He wanted to undress every woman he looked at. Mae comments that even when their father took them to the zoo, the only thing that interested him was the animals having sex. So for West marriage was an irrelevancy. It could only prevent him from achieving his aim of having a thousand women.

Albert DeSalvo, the Boston Strangler, who suffered from the same problem, and who once raped two women in the same afternoon, realised that there was something wrong with him, and begged the prison authorities to give him treatment. He recognised that to be capable of having sex a dozen or more times a day was not a sign of virility but an illness akin to alcoholism. As far as we know, West never even suspected that his raging desire for the opposite sex was in any way abnormal. He was like the man in the joke who was taking a Rorschach test and found that every pattern reminded him of sex, and who when the psychologist told him he was a sex maniac said: "Me a sex maniac? — who's been showing me the dirty pictures?"

Almost certainly, West married Rena because she wanted to get married, and he took the path of least resistance. This would also explain why, after the marriage, he treated her so badly. He felt she had trapped him.

After a brief "honeymoon" at Moorcourt Cottage — his parents naturally assumed that the baby Rena was carrying was Fred's — they moved to Scotland, to a small flat at 46 Hospital Street, Coatbridge. In *The Missing*, Andrew O'Hagan — who interviewed some of Rena West's Glasgow acquaintances — reports that West stayed behind in Much Marcle until the March of the following year, when Charmaine was born in the Alexander Hospital on March 22, 1963. The baby was originally called Mary, and christened in St Mary's Catholic Church, Coatbridge. At Fred's instigation, Rena wrote to her mother-in-law telling her that her baby had died in childbirth, and she had adopted a half-coloured child.

Sexually, they were not well suited. Fred's sexual demands were already peculiar; he wanted oral sex, bondage and probably (to judge by his later proclivities) sodomy. And in spite of her experience as a prostitute, Rena seems to have objected to this. What was inevitable was that Fred should have wanted sex at all hours of the day and night. "Normal sex" interested him only minimally. It was conducted without kisses or caresses, and was probably accompanied by a fantasy that he was raping her.

For a while, Fred and Rena seem to have split up, and she moved into the ground-floor flat of a tenement at 25 Savoy Street, in Glasgow. It was the worst kind of slum, and was about to be demolished. Many houses in this area had a "bin" instead of a flush toilet. At some time during this period, Rena went back to prostitution, probably at Fred's insistence. An old Irishwoman known as Auntie looked after Charmaine while Rena was away. Rena may have thought that Fred was interested only in the money she earned, failing to realise that the thought of her being possesssed by other men excited him.

Back home that Christmas, Fred hinted that he had become a pimp with a connection with the Glasgow gangs — in which there may have been an element of truth, since he apparently became a friend of the father of Rena's unborn child — the Pakistani pimp who remained her lover, and occasionally procured women for her complaisant husband without charging.

In fact, he was working as an ice cream seller, in a Mr Whippy van rented from Walls Ice Cream in Paisley. Anne Marie — who was born in July 1964 at Savoy Street — recalls how her father used to take her with him in his ice cream van, and how she slept in a cradle all day.

The job suited Fred, since it gave him an opportunity to meet teenage girls; his success in seduction seems to have been considerable. Looking at photographs of West, with his curly black hair and almost simian features, this is hard to understand. But he had always had the "gift of the gab", an easy charm that meant he found it easy to make friends.

He liked people because he liked impressing them; he wanted them to think well of him. (Mae describes how he would often engage tramps in conversation in Cromwell Street, then show them proudly all over his house.) With his soft West Country accent, he seemed sincere and trustworthy. Although short, he had broad, powerful shoulders; his best feature was his piercing blue eyes. And people who thought that he was a typical decent, hard-working countryman had no way of knowing that half his stories were lies, made up on the spur of the moment for effect, and then repeated until he half-believed them himself. His children are unananimous in saying that nothing he said could be taken on trust, because he lied so fluently and spontaneously. (His various confessions to the police make this apparent — probably no other killer has invented so freely or contradicted himself so often.) The blow on the head had turned him not merely into a sex maniac, but also into a mythomaniac.

But girls liked this short but powerfully-built young man with blue eyes and cheerful smile, who exuded an air of good nature. (It is surprising how many of his workmates later testified to his good nature — one said he was the sort of man everybody would like to invite into their home — and found it unbelievable that he could be a killer.) Fred liked to be liked; it was important to him that people thought him a "nice man." He was naturally polite, almost obsequious. So his success with women is not hard to explain.

This period in Glasgow was of central importance to his development. In Much Marcle he was not taken seriously, merely one of the local farm lads. In Glasgow he was the ice cream Casanova. To the teenage girls on the featureless estates, he must have seemed far more interesting and mature than their pimply male contemporaries with their Elvis Presley hair styles and lack of conversational expertise. Besides, he had a "place" — of a kind: the ice cream van. Suddenly he had nearly all the sex he wanted. The van was supposed to be returned by ten at night, but he was often out until four in the morning. He claimed on one occasion to have had sex with a girl in the middle of the Glasgow football stadium. This may have been fantasy, but there were plenty of local parks.

One writer, picking up on a suggestion by Rena's boyfriend John McLachlan, suggests that West may have begun murdering girls in Scotland, and burying their bodies in his vegetable patch at the end of the street. This seems to me to reveal a misunderstanding of West's character. Although he undoubtedly had some sinister perversions, like a taste for sadism and dismemberment, he also had plenty of outlets for his sex drives. West was not basically the rapist type. Like Rouse, the burning car murderer, he relied on his charm and his fluent tongue. Seduction satisfied his ego as much as his sex drive. And it was his ego and self-confidence that expanded during the Glasgow period. One girl who worked in a bottling factory became pregnant and had a son called Steven in 1966. Another of his illegitimate children was called Gareth.

The loser in all this was his wife. She was an irrelevancy, someone who had trapped him into marriage. Neighbours later told journalist Andrew O'Hagen that they seldom saw Fred at Savoy Street; he used the place mainly for sleeping. Rena struck them as very clean and very young, taking care of her two children, both dressed identically.

Left alone for long periods, Rena took to going to a cafe called the Victoria in Scotland Street. There she met two younger girls, Isa McNeill and Anna (known as Ann) McFall both factory workers, although Isa was unemployed at the time. The three soon began to meet regularly, and Rena asked Isa to move into their flat as a nanny — probably to alleviate her loneliness.

Isa McNeill remembers this period as the time Fred started being physically violent with his wife. Rena was a woman with a will of her own — particularly when she had been drinking — and Fred's reaction to her defiance was to punch her. He was always immensely possessive, to the degree of wanting to control the lives of those close to him — he even kept his two children in bunk beds covered with chicken wire, so they could not get out. But since he was away so much of the time, he could hardly expect Rena to remain in the flat all day. One day, Rena had dropped in on the neighbour who lived below on the ground floor, Sarah Mason, and while she was there Sarah's husband Norrie came home from the local betting shop with a young married man called John McLachlan. The two men had brought whisky and beer home with them, and sat drinking. Suddenly a face appeared at the window, glaring at Rena. When John opened the door Fred West stormed in, grabbed Rena, and dragged her upstairs, beating her as they went.

McLachlan had been attracted to the pretty blonde, and she seems to have felt the same. John McLachlan speculates that it was love and tenderness she was seeking, and that Fred made no attempt to supply these. So Rena began to go down to the betting shop when she knew John would be there, and they began an affair — although McLachlan claims that it was some time before they became lovers. Oddly enough, Fred West and John McLachlan remained on friendly terms; they played cards together in Fred's flat, and John even allowed West to use his allotment shed for assignations with women.

Rena in turn made a habit of slipping into the local park with John McLachlan. One evening Fred West saw them there "kissing and cuddling", and grabbed Rena from behind, hitting her. McLachlan hit Fred, who pulled out a knife and cut McLachlan across the stomach. McLachlan then attacked West and — by his own later account — gave him a beating. Fred soon gave way. But it did Rena no good — the next day she had a black eye and a broken tooth.

In spite of this, Rena continued her affair, often going around the pubs with McLachlan, Isa McNeill, and Isa's boyfriend John Trotter. She told McLachlan that Fred's sexual demands were "weird." Rena had always had a capacity for getting drunk, and this undoubtedly added to the instability of the marriage. The affair with McLachlan eventually broke up his own marriage.

Oddly enough, the teenager Ann McFall soon decided she was in love with Fred, his violence towards his wife notwithstanding. She came from a poverty-stricken home, and had often seen her mother beaten up; her brother spent a great deal of time in jail. So Ann was inured to domestic violence. She had had a boyfriend for a while, but he was accidentally electrocuted at work. Now she transferred her affections to Fred, who was becoming increasingly enraged with Rena — particularly when he found out that the "Fred" tattoo on Rena's arm had been inked over and replaced by "John." And Ann McFall, with the unconscious opportunism of young girls who need a lover, probably recognised that there was room for another woman in Fred's life.

Fred's problems came to a head when he accidentally killed a small boy, backing his ice cream van over him. The boy's father threatened to kill him. West was not charged with the child's death, but decided it was time to leave Glasgow and go back to his home county.

On December 11, 1965, Fred West returned to Gloucester by train with the two children, and stayed with his family at Much Marcle; Rena had decided not to accompany him. But she rejoined him two months later, on February 23, 1966.

Soon after, they moved to the Willows caravan site at the nearby village of Sandhurst. Rena again took a job in a cafe, while Fred found himself work in an abattoir. And this, I would suggest, was another turning point in his life, as far reaching in its consequences as the head accidents.

No one, as far as I know, has recognised the possible influence of the abattoir job on West's sexuality. Yet one thing is clear: that at some stage, West developed a morbid obsession with corpses and blood and dismemberment. There is no evidence that he had shown any such interest so far. But by 1969, three years later, a friend named Terry Crick, who shared his caravan for a time, talked about West's trade as an abortionist, and "gruesome polaroid photographs of bloodstained women."

"He laughed as he showed me the photos, as if they turned him on." And the body of Ann McFall, murdered in 1967, had been dismembered, and had the usual missing fingers and toes, as well as kneecaps.

The notion of being turned on by the sight of blood and dismembered carcases may seem incomprehensible. But it is a perversion that can be found in most textbooks In *The Sexual Anomalies and Perversions*, Magnus Hirschfeld notes: "Butchers and hunters are frequently represented in the list of murderers. In the course of their profession they lose the aversion to killing that the normal human being experiences, and in the act of killing animals they discover, in most cases by accident and to their own surprise — a usual feature in the acquirement of sexual perversions — *that killing gives them pleasure, and this arouses in them the desire to murder.*" (My italics.)

He goes on to cite one of the best known cases of the later 19th century, that of Eusebius Pieydagnelle.

"A man afflicted with the desire to kill is described in Emile Zola's La Bete Humaine.

"It is said that Zola used as his model the French murderer Eusebius Pieydagnelle, who was tried in 1871 for four murders. In the speech he addresed to the jury, a record of which is extant, he begged the jury to sentence him to death.

"He said that he would have killed himself but for the fact that he believed in a Beyond, and did not want to add a further sin to his score.

"Pieydagnelle told the jury that he came from highly respectable parents, and had had an excellent education. Unfortunately, opposite their house in Vinuville there was a butcher's shop kept by a M. Cristobal.

"The smell of fresh blood, the appetising meat, the bloody lumps — all this fascinated me, and I began to envy the butcher's assistant, because he could work at the block, with rolled-up sleeves and bloody hands.

"Then, in spite of his parents' opposition, he persuaded them to apprentice him to Cristobal. Here he drank blood in secret and wounded the cattle. He derived the greatest excitement when he was permitted to kill an animal himself.

"But the sweetest sensation is when you feel an animal trembling under your knife. The animal's departing life creeps along the blade right up to your hand. The mighty blow that felled the bullocks sounded like sweet music in my ears.

"Unfortunately for him, his father took him away from the butcher and apprenticed him to a notary. But it was too late. He was seized with a terrible depression, a deep melancholia, and since he could no longer kill animals, he began to kill people. Six times he committed murder under the compulsion of the same urge.

"He tried to isolate himself from the world, and lived in a cave in a wood. But it was all in vain; his impulse was stronger than he. His last victim was his first employer, M.Cristobal. The murderer then gave himself up.

"His first victim was a girl of 15, and he described his sensation when he killed her as follows:

'As I looked at the lovely creature my first thought was that I should like to kiss her. I bent down... But I paused — a stolen kiss is of no use. But I could not bring myself to wake her up. I looked at her lovely neck — and at that moment, the gleam of the kitchen knife that lay beside the girl caught my eye. Something drew me irresistibly towards the knife.' "

In a review of a book about the Yorkshire Ripper, *Somebody's Husband, Somebody's Son* (1984), by Gordon Burn, I wrote:

"How does a man acquire a taste for disembowelling women? I suspect the answer may be: all too easily. I read Burn's book on the Ripper on a train journey to London, en route to do a breakfast TV show. On my way back to Paddington station, I began to discuss the case with the hire-car driver, Andrew Fowler, who provided me with a hair-raising insight. Fowler told me that he had worked for two years in a slaughterhouse, because it paid so well. He had always been an animal lover, but found that killing cattle could be treated merely as a job. Then one day he began to look at horses and dogs with the thought: 'I wonder what it would be like to kill it?'

"He decided that it was time to change his job. Fowler also described to me a slaughterman who was not happy until he was covered from head to foot in blood; once he was in this state, his eyes began to bulge in an odd way . . ."

In *Psychopathia Sexualis*, Krafft-Ebing spends some time discussing cases of necrophilia and the mutilation of corpses. He speculates that this is a form of lust-murder, which is held in check by "a remnant of moral sense", so that the perpetrator prefers to attack corpses. And this judgement seems to be borne out by the case he proceeds to cite, that of the necrophile Sergeant Bertrand.

Bertrand, like West, suffered from "hypersexuality", a desire so powerful that it was almost impossible to satisfy. At 13, he masturbated while he imagined a roomfull of women, with whom he had sex before killing them. He began to mutilate the corpses of animals. Yet when he joined the army, he had sex with many girls, all of whom he satisfied normally.

One day, in a graveyard, he saw a half-filled grave where a woman had been buried. He made an excuse to get rid of a friend, then returned to the grave, exposed the corpse, and began to beat it with a spade. He was overheard, and had to flee. But two days later, he dug up the grave with his hands, then tore out the corpses abdomen. Subsequently, Bertrand often made love to corpses; in the case of one sixteen year old girl, "he tried on the corpse all the arts he had practised on his living mistresses." Then he ended by cutting up the corpse and tearing out the intestines.

After this, in March 1848, he made love to four female corpses, and ended by slitting their mouths and cutting off their hands and feet. Note that Bertrand's necrophilia began as a desire to make love to a corpse, but soon developed into the need to mutilate and tear out intestines.

When the sex impulse is freed from all restraints, it tends to develop into sadism. Here, then, we can at last begin to understand something of Fred West's appalling secret, and why he told his son Stephen: "I only made love to them when they were dead."

Corpses, and the dismembering of corpses, filled him with excitement. This is not speculation; it is something we know, from the missing fingers, toes and kneecaps in corpse after corpse, and the removal of the foetus from the two pregnant women he killed.

What we do not know is whether West had any tendency to necrophilia and sadism before he became a butcher. We know, from Rena's comment to John McLachlan, that he had "weird" sexual tastes, such as bondage, but this is not quite the same. We also know that when he married Rena, he struck her as fairly normal; it was only later that he began to beat her and to make "weird" sexual demands.

It seems, then, that Fred West's sexual perversion became slowly more obsessive in the period following his marriage, and the evidence suggests that the necrophilia and desire to mutilate corpses began during his period as a butcher.

That his marriage was as unstable as ever is shown by the fact that Rena left Fred more than once after moving down to join him in Much Marcle. It must be admitted that, chronologically speaking, this part of the story is a mess — three different sources, including the Media Information Reports, issued by the police, give different and incompatible stories. But the general outline is clear.

In the spring of 1966, Rena returned to Glasgow, and when she came back, her friends Isa McNeill and Ann McFall accompanied her, possibly to entice her back.

Fred had told her that he had found a house big enough for all of them. Ann McFall, whose home life had become increasingly miserable since her brother came out of jail, was delighted to escape from Glasgow — and probably at the thought of getting close to Fred. Isa was also full of optimism — she believed they could both make a new start in Gloucester, and find themselves decent jobs.

Rena and her friends travelled by train to Gloucester, and were met by Fred in his butcher's lorry, full of hides and stinking bones. But it seemed that all the talk about a house big enough for all of them was another example of Fred's mythomania; he was still living in the caravan site at Sandhurst. And soon four adults and two children were sharing a cramped caravan.

For Isa and Ann it must have been an immense disappointment. The Wests had a bed in the end compartment, separated from the rest of the caravan by a screen. The two children slept on beds that pulled down from the wall. Isa and Ann slept on two settees on either side of the kitchen table. The girls were trapped in the caravan.

Sandhurst was three miles from Gloucester, and they didn't have the bus fare to go in and out regularly. Even Rena no longer had work. In effect, the caravan was a prison camp. Fred even warned Rena not to go off the site while he was at work. It was as if he wanted to keep total control over his "family." And the beatings administered to Rena became more violent — Isa and Anne often left the caravan to get out of hearing, taking the children with them.

Finally, Isa and Rena decided to return to Glasgow. Isa rang the Victoria Cafe from a public phone booth, leaving a message for John McLachlan. When he rang back, she told him they wanted to escape. He agreed to drive down and collect them — by the telephone kiosk, at a time when Fred would be at work. But Ann McFall could not resist telling Fred, and he was there waiting when the red Mini arrived with John McLachlan and Isa's boyfriend John Trotter.

There was a noisy scene — so noisy the neighbours rang the police. Rena wanted to take the children, but Fred was determined to keep them — he clung on tightly to Charmaine, even when John McLachlan punched him in the stomach.

Isa begged Ann to join them, but Ann — clinging to Anne Marie — said she would stay and get a job in Gloucester.

Obviously, this situation is what she had been hoping and planning for. She had probably warned Fred so that Rena could not take the children away, and she would have an excuse to stay behind as their nanny. It is difficult to know why Fred refused to let the children go, since a few weeks after Rena had left he was applying to have them taken into care. But West seldom behaved rationally; he was driven by some obscure compulsion for control over others — the same compulsion that would later turn 25 Cromwell Street into a kind of prison camp.

Ann McFall soon became Fred's mistress — probably the same day they were left alone. Meanwhile, Isa and Rena returned to Glasgow, where they spent the night in the hired car, having nowhere else to go. The next day, they found a flat together. But Rena was miserable about leaving her children behind. She begged Isa to return with her and help her get them back, but Isa was planning marriage to John Trotter, and had no wish to leave Glasgow.

Finally, in July 1966, Rena went alone — and found, as she had half-expected, that Fred and Ann were sleeping together. At least Fred made no objection when Rena took the children with her to the Watersmead caravan site at the village of Brockworth. But she was jealous of Ann, and to spite her, stole some of her belongings.

After this, she returned to her old trade of burglary, and broke into another caravan on the site. Then she hastened back to Scotland. And it was to bring her back that a young Woman Police Constable named Hazel Savage flew to Glasgow.

It was on this trip that Rena told Hazel Savage that her husband was a sexual pervert who was probably insane. In court on November 29, 1966, Hazel Savage saw Fred West for the first time — a scruffy, loutish looking man whose most striking feature was his blue eyes.

West admitted that he was living with Ann McFall, which supported Rena's defence that she had stolen out of spite. Fred told the court that he was paying Ann McFall's fare back to Glasgow. And when the defence solicitor pleaded that if Rena was sent to prison, her children would have to be taken into care, she was given three years probation. But Fred did not pay Ann's fare back to Scotland, and Rena moved back to the Brockworth caravan site.

The complicated three-way relationship seems to have continued, although Ann found herself a room in Gloucester.

Like Fred, Ann McFall seems to have been

something of a mythomaniac. After Rena and Isa had returned to Glasgow, she had written telling them that she had found a wonderful man, and that they were going to live in the attractive house whose photograph she enclosed. (In fact, it was a house near the caravan site.) That lie was exposed when Rena returned and found her sharing Fred's bed. But in the spring of 1967, when Ann discovered she was pregnant, she decided to tell her mother the truth, and wrote to her telling her that she was in love with Fred.

From the enthusiasm of her description, it may be inferred that Fred was not beating her as he beat Rena, and that possibly he felt a real attachment to her — he was later to claim that she was the only woman he had ever loved. But although Fred had enjoyed having a mistress who was eight years his junior, all this talk of divorce and remarriage was undoubtedly too much. He was still driven by his sinister compulsions — rape and dismemberment. And some time in July 1967, he murdered her in the caravan where they had lived together, and buried her nearby.

When her skeleton was found sixteen years later, in June 1994, there was an eight month old foetus nearby, and a length of dressing gown cord tied around the wrists.

West claimed that he had killed her in the course of a quarrel, but this fails to explain the cord. What had happened, almost certainly, is that West had tied her up to indulge in bondage sex, probably with flogging or whipping, and became carried away.

Then he was able to indulge his morbid dreams of necrophily and dismemberment. He cut off her fingers and toes, and disposed of them later elsewhere.

It is possible that this dismemberment was carried out in the abandoned farm building that he later described to his son Stephen.

He placed the body parts in plastic bags, and drove towards his home in Much Marcle. It was a journey of twenty miles or so, and unless he made a long detour, would have involved driving through the centre of Gloucester. With so much digging in front of him, and with the short nights of July, he could not afford to set out too late, so he must have driven through Gloucester at a time when his van might have been stopped by the police.

His destination was a large cornfield, Fingerpost Field, a mile from Much Marcle. Behind it there stood a coppice, which Fred knew from his courting days.

There, in the middle of the night, he dug a five foot hole, and lowered the remains into it.

Digging and filling in the grave must have taken him most of the night. We know nothing of West's state of mind following the murder. But one thing is obvious: that he must have believed that he was likely to be caught. Most first-time murderers feel like this, expecting a knock on the door at any moment. Ann had friends and relatives in Scotland; they might report her disappearance to the police.

Only as weeks, and then months, went by would he begin to feel relaxed again.

5
VANISHINGS

Now that her rival had conveniently vanished, Rena moved back in with Fred. She probably took it for granted that Ann had simply gone back to Scotland. And West probably found it a relief to have his wife back again — it made him seem more normal and respectable.

Only weeks after Ann McFall's death, in September 1967, they moved again, this time to Lakehouse caravan site, near the village of Bishop's Cleeve, three miles north of Cheltenham. Fred found himself a labouring job at a mill that manufactured flour and animal feed. Howard Sounes visited the site, and describes it: "The caravans were grouped around the lake... Fred rented No. 17 which, like most of the caravans, did not have any wheels, and was set on a concrete stand. It had a low garden and was surrounded by a low wooden fence.

"The caravan itself was not the most modern or best-kept on the site. It was slightly shabby, about twenty feet long, built of plywood and painted a cream colour. There were two bedrooms, a dining area, and a stove with a shiny metal chimney. A large septic tank on the site provided for the sewage and toilet facilties. The lake was filled in during the late 1980s; one resident of the site told a reporter: 'God knows what's in there' "

Sounes also learned, from a man who had lived on the site at the time, that while Fred was working nights, men came to the caravan — always the same men. And unless she had a series of lovers, it seemed clear that she was working as a prostitute.

West was probably glad of the extra cash — he was heard to grumble about how little he was paid. The same informant told Sounes that Fred had claimed he was used to riding big motor bikes — 400cc — and that he had ridden in the Isle of Man race.

West never, during his whole life, lost this tendency to lie simply for the pleasure of it, just as he stole. West also took sexually explicit pictures of Rena — just as he would later of Rose — and was also seen sitting with Charmaine, who was wearing nothing on her lower half, on his naked lap, rubbing her against him.

After he and Rena had separated yet again in early 1969, West met a young man called Terry Crick who needed somewhere to live with his girlfriend, and invited them to share the caravan.

Crick told a reporter: "He showed me the garage next door. It was cold and eerie. The place was dirty and damp, and there were stains all over the place."

Fred then opened a dusty cupboard, and pulled out a tray contaning an oxyacetylene burner, a large knife, two bottles of antiseptic, and a ten inch tube with a corkscrew at one end. Under these tools were photographs of bloodstained women. Crick said: "I felt they turned him on."

West went on to explain exactly how he performed abortions, and asked Crick to help him recruit girls who needed his services.

"I took him to the Full Moon pub in Cheltenham that night, and watched him leave with a girl. I packed my stuff the same night and left the site."

Stephen West would say of his father: "He had a thing about women's bodies — he was into the internal bits — and he wanted to get as close as he could. He really wanted to get inside them... I know he wanted a tiny little pencil camera, the ones they use on pregnant women. He wanted to look at the womb because it was something he didn't have."

Since West's days — after a few hours sleep — were free, he earned extra money by doing jobs on the site, such as maintainence for the owner. He also did some building work in Gloucester, at a cafe called The Breakfast Bar, better known as the Pop-In, in Southgate Street.

Sounes describes it as a seedy dive used as a gathering point for petty criminals and drop-outs.

It was also popular with teenagers. Fifteen-year-old Mary Bastholm had worked there as a waitress since she left school. She was small — only 5' 3" — and slim, and her shoulder-length blonde hair was parted in the middle.

On the snowy night of January 6, 1968, Mary waited at a bus stop in Bristol Road, on her way to see her boyfriend, who lived at the village of Hardwicke.

This was the last time she was seen. Her disappearance led to a widespread search of surrounding fields, and Scotland Yard was called in. Soon after this, her parents received an anonymous message, telling them to place an advertisement in the Skyrack Express, in Tadcaster, Yorkshire, saying that they forgave her for running away. They did this, but heard no word from Mary.

One man went to the police to report that he had seen her four or five times in the autumn before she disappeared.

He was a 45-year-old joiner named Vincent Oakes,

who lived a few doors away from Mary's home. She had, he said, always been with the same man, and once he saw her sitting in a car with him.

In 1994, when newspaper photographs of Fred West began to appear, Vincent Oakes told the *Daily Mirror* that this was the man he had seen with Mary.

"It was always parked in the same place, about two or three hundred yards from her home. I thought it strange that she didn't acknowledge me. I'm certain it was Mary, and I'm 99.9% sure the man was Fred."

What seems to be implied is that Mary was having an affair with West, who was then in his mid-twenties. But if she was having an affair with West, why should he kill her for sex? The alternative suggestion is that she might have been pregnant by West, and that he felt she had to "disappear", like Ann McFall. (In fact, Mary had been seen on a number of occasions with a girl answering to Ann McFall's description, and may have met Fred through her.)

When questioned by the police about the murders, West refused to discuss Mary Bastholm. This in itself sounds strange — if he had not killed her, he might be expected to say so. But to his son Stephen, he almost admitted killing Mary.

Stephen told the *News of the World*: "One time I mentioned I had seen the brother of one of the victims, Mary Bastholm, on the TV." I said: "You don't know anything about it, do you?", and he looked at the ground. When I told him they were going to go into a cafe to knock a wall down which he'd built, he said: 'It's a waste of time looking in there.' I went really cold. I didn't know what he meant. I said: 'Why's that?' "

"He said: 'They are going to have to carry on finding out themselves. I'm fed up with helping them.' "

"He kept saying: 'I'll be out of here in 12 years and we'll all go back to live again in Cromwell Street. If they find any more bodies I'll never get out.' " But West told his counsellor, Janet Leach, that Rose had murdered Mary Bastholm. Chronologically, this is impossible, for he had met Rose soon after her fifteenth birthday, which was in November 1968, and Mary had vanished ten months earlier. But then, West told Janet Leach that Rose had killed most of the victims, so his accusation of Rose seems to at least suggest that he was involved in the disappearance of Mary Bastholm — otherwise, why not flatly deny knowing anything about it? If he did kill Mary Bastholm, then the likeliest site for her burial is Fingerpost Field, where he had already buried Ann McFall, or the adjoining Letter Box Field, where he would later bury Rena. Both fields are huge — about 13 acres — and only a small proportion has been searched. Fred was to tell his counsellor Janet Leach that he had buried Mary in a field.

During 1968, West had changed his job. He had been dismissed from the Oldacre corn mill in Bishop's Cleeve on suspicion of stealing money. He had also been in trouble for stealing a blank cheque from a house where he was working in Cheltenham, and forging a cheque for £10 to buy a record player. For this he was fined £20. Now he began to drive a baker's van. On November 29, 1968, Rose Letts, who lived in Bishop's Cleeve, turned fifteen and left school, and went to work in a bread shop in Cheltenham. She later told her daughter Mae how she had met Fred.

"I was standing at a bus stop when I noticed this man looking at me. I didn't take to him at all — he was dirty and had work clothes, and looked quite old." The man sat next to her on the bus and started a conversation. Minutes later, he asked her to go out with him.

"He was like a tramp, a real mess, and I said 'no.' I thought that was the end of that." But she saw him again at the bus stop, and he again sat next to her, and asked her out. Again she declined. One day, a woman came into the bread shop and handed Rose some small gift, which she said a man had asked her to pass on to her. (Rose could not recall what the present was.) Then Fred himself came into the shop, and shouted: "The Swallow — 8 pm." That was her local pub in Bishop's Cleeve. Out of curiosity, she went along. They had a drink together — Rose was allowed in a pub, but not to drink alcohol, so presumably she drank something non-alcoholic. West now exercised his famous "gift of the gab."

His brother was to tell a reporter that even in his teens, Fred had a remarkable ability to pick up girls — if one attracted him, he walked straight over and spoke to her.

Rose found his fluency impressive — and no doubt believed most of his lies — his own colourful version of his past, which probably included his story of how, after the motor cycle accident, he had been assumed to be dead; placed on a mortuary slab, he been awakened by the cold.

Rose was lonely. At 15, she was overweight, and not particularly pretty. She told police later that she had lost her virginity when she was 14 — that she had been raped during Christmas 1968 by an older man who had offered her a lift after a Christmas party.

Whether or not she found Fred sexually attractive, she would have been flattered by his attention, and his tendency to treat her as an adult — not as the schoolgirl she still felt she was.

At this time, Rena had left him again, and Fred was living in the caravan with the two children. He told Rose that his wife had returned to Scotland, where she was workng as a prostitute; in fact, she was still living near Cheltenham, and would face magistrates in March 1969 for defrauding the Social Security.

Rose Letts allowed herself to be persuaded to visit the caravan, and met the children. At this time, she claims, she was by no means the only teenage girl to go to the caravan. "Fred had many babysitters — a lot of them were girls from my school — and, according to Rose, "most of them were sleeping with Fred."

Evidently West's gifts as a Casanova had not deteriorated since Glasgow. Rose does not tell us how long it took Fred to persuade her into bed, but on her previous showing — and his own record — it was probably the first time.

Soon she felt sufficiently possessive about him to chuck them all out, together with the trunk of women's underwear he had at the back of the caravan.

In an interview soon after Rose's arrest in 1994, her brother Graham stated that after meeting Fred, Rose became "sex mad" — implying that she had earlier been an innocent schoolgirl. But after the trial, a fuller — and altogether more sinister — picture began to emerge. As one journalist — Paul Henderson — put it: "Rose's upbringing had been, in many ways, even more perverse than that of (Fred) West."

Rosemary Pauline Letts was born on November 29, 1953, in Barnstaple, North Devon, and spent most of her childhood in a small council house divided into two flats at Morwenna Park in the uninspiring village of Northam. The family was chronically short of money. Her father, Bill Letts, was an electrical engineer in the navy. He was also, to all intents and purposes, a madman. In fact, Bill Letts belonged to the type that A.E. Van Vogt has called "the Right Man" or "the Violent Man" — the Right Man because he refuses to admit that he could ever be in the wrong, and the Violent Man because if he is challenged by anyone he can bully, he explodes into disproportionate violence.

His mainspring is his self-esteem — his desire to be liked and respected and admired. But as often as not, he possesses few qualities that would bring him admiration or respect. So he compensates by behaving like a dictator in his own family.

Bill Letts was an extreme of this type. With his wife and seven children, he was a brutal bully. The least sign of disobedience or contradiction threw him into a blind rage in which he struck out.

The children had to do the housework and the gardening, and if everything was not perfect, there were beatings. His mild-mannered wife Daisy, who had been a housemaid when they met, had been literally battered into submission until she was terrified of answering back.

Bill Letts was worse than a domestic tyrant; he was a sadistic maniac. His son Andrew recollected: "If he felt we were in bed too late, he would throw a bucket of cold water over us. He would order us to dig the garden, and that meant the whole garden. Then he would inspect it like an army officer, and if he was not satisfied, we would have to do it all over again.

"We would have to clean the house, and if he found a speck of dust, we would have to clean it again.

"We were not allowed to speak and play like normal children. If we were noisy, he would go for us with a belt or a chunk of wood. He would beat you black and blue until mum got in between us. Then she would get a good hiding."

It was so bad that his wife even had to call the police on more than one occasion. In fact, Bill Letts had been diagnosed a schizophrenic with paranoid tendencies. And his brutality had reduced his wife to such a state of depression that when she was pregnant with Rose, she received Electro-Convulsive Therapy. But Rose, the youngest of the family, managed to escape the beatings.

Andrew commented: "She was a lovely little thing with a pony tail, who was pampered by mum and dad." But this quiet, dark-eyed, olive-skinned girl, was not the type to be battered into submission. Rose was a survivor. She escaped beatings by quietly doing everything her father ordered her to, never showing the slightest rebelliousness. "She knew how to manipulate dad," said Andrew. So her father gave her the affection that he denied to her six brothers and sisters.

Nevertheless, Rose showed one of the classic symptoms of an emotionally deprived childhood, rocking herself back and forward, with her thumb in her mouth — her sisters complained that she kept them awake doing this even when she was a schoolgirl.

In some ways, the Letts household bore an ominous resemblance to 25 Cromwell Street. Bill Letts made sure that his family kept to itelf. The children were not allowed to have to friends. He was probably afraid that his insane violence might come to the attention of the authorities.

Even so, the screams that issued from their tiny flat alerted neighbours in Northam and caused gossip.

Bill Letts began to make a habit of locking doors and windows before he beat his family, so the screams would not carry. Finally, the elder daughters, Patricia and Joyce, were taken into care by the local authorities. At that point, Bill Letts moved his family to a small flat in Plymouth, and took a job at the dockyard.

In 1966, when Rose was twelve, Bill Letts moved again, this time to a three-bedroomed council house in Bishop's Cleeve, in Gloucestershire. Age was not making him any less brutal; one neighbour, Rita New, decribed how he had strode out and grabbed his wife by the hair as she chatted over the fence to neighbours; she was breaking the basic rule — that the family had no outside contact.

"He dragged her indoors by the hair, and the screams were terrible. The police were called, but little happened."

Money was still tight, and it was necessary for both parents to work. While Bill and Daisy Letts were out in the evenings, Rosie, who was now the eldest left at home, had to bath and look after the younger children. She enjoyed this role — even at school, she was usually to be seen followed by a crowd of younger children, like a mother duck with its brood. But as her figure developed, she was also becoming aware of her sexuality.

After baths, she would walk around the house naked. Soon she was climbing into bed with eleven-year-old Graham, and playing with his genitals.

"Things happened which did nothing for me", Graham was later to admit. And Bill Letts also seems to have become aware of his daughter's burgeoning sexuality. He had already an unpleasant reputation for being interested in young children. Now he turned his attention to his daughter.

It may well have been to her father that Rose Letts lost her virginity at fourteen. In early 1968, Daisy

Letts snapped, and decided to leave her husband. She and the children moved to a chicken farm to live in a cottage; they had, according to Graham, no money, no furniture and no clothes; Mrs Letts earned a little by cleaning. Yet oddly enough, Rose decided after a few weeks to return to her father.

Other family members believe that this was because they were involved in an incestuous relationship. Her brother-in-law Jim Tyler believes that there was also an incestuous relationship with her grandfather, who lived nearby.

"There was something about her father and grandfather that just wasn't right."

A.E.Van Vogt noticed an interesting thing about "Right Men"; they may treat their wives appallingly, beating them, being unfaithful and even leaving them destitute; yet if she deserts him, he experiences a total moral collapse. The reason should be obvious. His self-esteem fantasy, his notion of being an "important person", is based on his wife's total obedience. If she revolts, she has undermined his sand castle of illusion; under such circumstances, Right Men have been known to commit suicide. But in this case, Bill Letts was saved by his daughter, who lost no time stepping into her mother's shoes.

Eventually, Daisy and the other children returned to Bill Letts. When it happened a second time, Rose also decided to go with her mother and brothers. But she had played her part; she had supported her father during that first crucial period. That she decided not to stay with him the second time may well be because she had already met Fred West.

On the second occasion, the family went to stay with Rose's elder sister Glenys, who was married to a motor mechanic named Jim Tyler. Tyler owned a roadside snack bar, and Rose began to work for him.

Tyler told Paul Henderson: "I would go there at four in the afternoon to find the hatch down and Rose in a lorry with a driver."

On one occasion, she returned in a car with a man driving a big Austin Princess; she explained that he had just given her a lift into town to buy some essentials that they had run out of.

Tyler also claims: "Around that time the police also picked her up for street-walking in Cheltenham. She was only 15." Tyler recounts how one night, he heard Rose crying in her bedroon, and went in to see what was the matter. Rose said she was lonely, and put her arms round Tyler. Then she told him how lucky Glenys was to be married to him, and ran her hand inside his thigh. Tyler hastily excused himself and left.

Rose's interest in older men became apparent. She would come home at 10 or 11 at night with a guy in his 30s', said her brother in law. This, of course, was only possible because they were not living at home with Bill Letts.

Paul Henderson insists that, according to his information, Rose did not meet Fred West at a bus stop — she was offered a lift by him in his van on the Stoke road, and accepted.

Henderson suggests that she told the other version because it sounded more "respectable" at a time when she was trying to insist on her innocence.

Whatever the truth, Rose lost no time in allowing herself to be seduced by West in his caravan. She even gave up her job in the bread shop in order to become the nanny of his children while he was at work. Her parents continued to believe she was still at work in Cheltenham; but the money she gave them on Fridays was given to her by West.

Eventually, Rose decided to take Fred home and

introduce him to her family. The result — predictably — was an explosion. Bill Letts later claimed that he disliked Fred because West was too old, and was coarse. Daisy Letts explained: "Dad said he did not want that gypsy anywhere near his daughter." The real reason was undoubtedly frantic jealousy.

Bill Letts may also have recognised Fred as a pathological liar. He boasted about the prosperous business he had left behind in Scotland, and the caravan site he owned, while it was perfectly obvious that he was living in a caravan because he had no money.

The conflicts were bitter and violent; when they found out that she was working for West as a nanny, Rose was ordered never to go near West's caravan again. She ignored this, and went on seeing him in secret. Unlike Rena (and possibly Ann McFall), Rose had no objections to Fred's sex games — to being tied up and tying Fred up, to beating and being beaten.

He also persuaded her to have sex with other men while he watched. The highly-sexed teenager needed no encouraging. She was already developing into a nymphomaniac. Bill Letts found about all this rather belatedly — in the summer of 1969 — and went to the Social Services to complain that his daughter was having sex with an older man. Rose was placed in care in Cheltenham.

When she heard that her mother and father had separated again after Bill had beat his wife worse than usual, she moved in to live with her mother for a while. Fred, meanwhile, was again in trouble with the police for petty offences, including stealing a tax disc, and failing to pay fines for past offences. He was fined another £20 for stealing from his employer, and given a six months suspended sentence.

When Bill Letts found out that Rose was seeing Fred again, he appeared at West's caravan, shouting and theatening to cut him into pieces. West took all this calmly, obviously feeling that Bill Letts was the least of his problems.

But in November 1969, Rose was placed in care again. Rena returned briefly to Fred, but stayed only three days.

Fred, meanwhile, was sent to prison for non-payment of fines. Charmaine and Rose were placed in custody again. But the social services were only able to keep her for a few weeks; as soon as she was sixteen, she was allowed to walk out.

There was another violent quarrel at home, and the police were called in. Rose was told that she could stay only on condition that she promised never to see West again. She seems to have made the promise in order to have somewhere to stay until Fred came out of prison. But the moment he was released, she left home, and moved into his caravan.

At home she was treated like a child; she was anxious to begin living as an adult — even if it meant putting up with Fred's desire to tie her up and flog her. Bill Letts was not finished; more complaints led to Rose being taken into custody and medically examined, when it was discovered she was pregnant.

Her father agreed to take her into his home again provided she had the pregnancy terminated. When Rose refused, he finally decided to leave her to go to the devil in her own way. Which was exactly what Rose proceeded to do.

Life with Fred West was hard. He had very little money, and was constantly in trouble with the police. And Rose, at sixteen, found it fatiguing work looking after two children — particularly since both were accustomed to freedom. The children in turn resented being "bossed" by a girl who was obviously many years younger than their mother. Anne Marie, who enjoyed a particularly close relationship with her father, resented the interloper, but said nothing; Charmaine, on the other hand, made it quite clear that she detested Rose, and had no hesitation in telling her so.

In the spring of 1970, the West family, including an obviously pregnant Rose, moved into Gloucester — number 10 Midland Road — an area that had once been a pleasant middle-class neighbourhood, but had now slipped into decline. On October 17, 1970, Rose gave birth to a daughter whom she named Heather Ann. By then they had moved a few doors down the street to 25 Midland Road.

Fred took a job — poorly paid as usual — with a tyre firm, and lost no time in trying to swindle them by presenting an order for five tyres worth £10 each. These he took away and sold second-hand. It was a poorly conceived crime, for the firm was bound to become suspicious when they tried to collect the money. (This lack of foresight is characteristic of people who have suffered damage to the prefrontal cortex of the brain.) West tried to escape the consequences by leaving the firm, and taking a job with his Polish landlord, Frank Zygmunt, who owned several properties in the area.

Soon West was in trouble for stealing another tax disc, and was summoned to appear in court. Then his previous employer caught up with him for the tyre swindle. West tried blaming Rena for the theft of the tax disc — he always clutched at the nearest excuse, no matter how unlikely — but the magistrates decided that he was a habitual rogue, and gave him a sentence of four months. His earlier six-month sentence — suspended on condition that he stayed out of trouble — was added to this. Soon after Christmas 1970, West went to prison.

For seventeen-year-old Rose, it must have been a miserable New Year; it was snowing, and she had little or no money. Her response was to behave like her father, and lose control every time she felt frustrated. Anne Marie usually escaped beatings by remaining quiet, but the more rebellious Charmaine received harsh treatment — and compounded the offence by refusing to cry, determined not to surrender when Rose beat her. Anne Marie recalls Charmaine being tied to a bed, and a neighbour's child, Tracey Giles, burst into the kitchen one day to find Charmaine standing on a stool with her hands tied behind her, while Rose menaced her with a wooden spoon.

Both children had been ordered to call Rose "mum", but even Anne Marie displayed passive resistance. Rose made them do the household chores — exactly as her own brothers and sisters had done — "and if you didn't do them right", Anne Marie recollected, "she erupted." It is a phenomenon familiar to psychologists — the ill-treated child who grows up to behave exactly like those who had ill-treated her.

Rose's increasing dislike of Charmaine is apparent from one of the letters she wrote to Fred in jail. "Darling, about Char. I think she likes to be handled rough. But darling, why do I have to be the one to do it. I would keep her for her own sake, if it wasn't for the rest of the children. You can see Char coming out in Anna now. And I hate it." She signed herself "Your ever worshipping wife", and Fred signed his own clumsy and mis-spelled missive "Your ever worshipping husband." The notion that any child can "like" being treated rough is so absurd that it can only be understood as an excuse for ill-treatment.

The children visited their father in prison — by May he had been moved to the Leyhill Open Prison, and Anne Marie recalls a sports day in which she took part in an egg and spoon race. On June 15, Rose applied to visit him again with the two children, but there is no record of it actually happening.

What is certain is that Charmaine West vanished some time in the summer of 1971. Anne Marie recalls returning home from school one day and asking where Charmaine was; Rose told her that Charmaine's real mother had come to take her away.

Tracey Giles's mother Shirley took her eight-year-old daughter back to visit her friend Charmaine in Midland Road some time that summer, and Tracey was upset to be told that Charmaine had left. (Rose commented: "bloody good riddance.") Shirley Giles was unable to remember the date, but she was so impressed by a model matchstick caravan that Fred made for Rose that she wrote to Fred in prison to ask him to make a similar one. This leaves no doubt that Charmaine's disappearance took place while Fred West was still in prison, and that therefore it was Rose who killed her.

The prosecution at the trial claimed that Rose West killed Charmaine some time between the visit in May and Fred's release from prison on June 25, 1971. If so, it seems likely that she simply lost her temper, and went further than usual in beating or throttling her. She was, as Anne Marie said, a woman entirely without self-control; when she lost her temper, she became a kind of maniac.

In *An Evil Love*, Geoffrey Wansell suggests another theory. He believes that Charmaine was raped by her father after Fred West came out of prison, and that probably Rose participated, as she participated in

Anne Marie's rape two years later. When, shortly after the discovery of the body, West was asked whether sex or bondage had anything to do with Charmaine's death, he refused to answer, but nodded. Wansell goes on to speculate that Charmaine may have been accidentally suffocated by a gag, or that she was killed because she threatened to tell her mother about the rape.

In view of the evidence of Shirley Giles that Charmaine had already vanished while West was still in prison, this scenario seems far-fetched. The dates alone suggest that Rose West, and Rose West alone, murdered her step-daughter.

So it seems likely that when Fred West came out of prison on June 24 (having gained a third remission for good conduct), his first task was to take the body of his first wife's child from wherever Rose had concealed it, and to bury it outside in the back yard — later, when he returned to the house to do building work, he reburied it under the kitchen floor, where it was eventually found twenty-three years later. Where had Rose hidden it? Traces of coal found with the body suggest that Charmaine was concealed under the coal in the coal cellar.

Howard Sounes has suggested that this was the point where Fred West told his wife about the murder of Ann McFall, and possibly of Mary Bastholm. But surely it is far more likely that Rose already knew that her husband was a murderer, and that this is why she was so certain of his co-operation in burying Charmaine when he came out of prison? They now shared the secret that the other was a murderer.

This, I would suggest, is one of the main psychological keys to the case. The criminal psychologist Oliver James is surely correct when he says that the incest in West's family, and particularly the incest with his mother, caused a fundamental breakdown of inhibitions, which in turn led to a kind of moral nihilism. It was this, and the "hypersexuality" caused by the head accidents, that turned West into a killer.

Rose's own incest with her father, and her increasing nymphomania, created a similar situation. Rose was one of Maslow's "dominant women", with an almost obessive interest in sex. She loved giving herself to virile lovers, particularly blacks, but she also loved to make love to young girls as if she was a sex-hungry male, kissing them, caressing their breasts and performing oral sex.

It is true that all this does not amount to a capacity to kill. But to know that the man she was in love with — and whom she regarded as a father figure — had already murdered his pregnant mistress was a traumatic piece of knowledge with which she had to come to terms. Fred was capable of murder. He was also capable of sudden insane rages — like her own father. Once she had accepted this, and decided that she still loved him, she had condoned murder. She had also condoned her own tendency to lose control and give way to explosions of violent temper. So when she killed Charmaine — probably seizing her by the throat and throttling her, as she later throttled Stephen until he lost consciousnessness — she had overcome all her inhibitions and taboos about violence. It is doubtful whether she intended to kill Charmaine, and virtually certain that the death was not preplanned. Stephen remarks of her: "Mum had no self-control. She would just flip and have no real idea of what she was doing ... (She) would hit out with anything she could lay her hands on ... If she'd had a sledgehammer in her hands she'd have belted you with it. A rolling pin was one of her favourites.

She would just lash out and you'd be sent flying."

So Charmaine's death was probably a kind of accident. But when Rose found that the child she had come to hate was dead she probably said: "Bloody good riddance."

It was in every way a pointless and stupid murder. It is virtually certain that Rena had already called on her and offered to take the children away — Anne Marie says so. Why did she refuse? Almost certainly because Anne Marie was her father's favourite, and because without Anne Marie, her own hold over Fred West would be greatly reduced. So she decided to keep both children — then, in a fit of fury, killed Charmaine.

Now she and Fred had crossed the same Rubicon, broken the same ultimate taboo. And when it came to satisfying her nymphomania with young girls, it made them a uniquely dangerous team — a sex maniac married to a nymphomaniac, both of whom lacked the usual inhibitions about killing.

Even in burying his daughter, Fred West seems to have been unable to resist indulging his morbid obsession with dismemberment. When Charmaine's body was found her kneecaps, as well as bones of the fingers and toes, were missing. They may have got lost in transferring the skeleton from one grave to another; but since so many other bodies lacked the same bones, this seems unlikely.

At some time in 1971, Rose decided to leave Fred. She would later claim that they quarrelled and he tried to strangle her. But the real motive, almost certainly, is that she was becomingly increasingly disillusioned with him. She had started by admiring him because he seemed so self-confident, and boasted about his success in Scotland. Then she had to accept that he was simply a pathological liar and an incompetent petty crook. His six months in jail made her miss him; but once he was back, it was impossible to overlook the fact that he was a thoroughly unadmirable character.

The fact that he insisted that she sleep with other men — while he watched — may also have soured their relation. Oddly enough, both Fred and Rose were at bottom conventional; Rose, between bouts of nymphomania, wanted to be a normal housewife, while Fred wanted to be a paterfamilias, the master of his own home. But Fred had no desire to allow Rose to become a normal housewife; watching his wife being possessed by other men had become one of his basic sexual needs. And his sexual abnormality meant that he was an unsatisfactory lover; his idea of lovemaking was simply to climb on top of her without any preliminaries, and reach a climax after a few minutes — sometimes seconds — of thrusting. Rose liked to be caressed and excited, but Fred only wanted to be excited by the woman he was about to enter. The very idea of oral sex, which Rose loved, revolted him. For someone as insatiable as Rose, Fred was a most unsatisfying lover.

Bill and Daisy Letts were startled when Rose arrived on their doorstep in Bishop's Cleeve carrying her baby. They had been to see her once or twice while Fred had been in jail, and been disturbed by her thinness, and the squalor of her flat. Her mother was also shocked by the coarseness and foul language she had picked up from her husband. Now she proposed to return home, all Bill Letts's deep resentment — the resentment of a jealous lover who has been rejected for another man — surfaced, and he told her that she would have to lie in the bed she had made for herself. But Fred arrived shortly after, and invited her home with the curious words: "Come

on, Rosie, you know what we've got between us."
And when Rose resisted, he warned her that unless
she came back, her place in his bed would be taken
by someone else within hours. She knew him well
enough to know that this was no idle threat. But
before capitulating, she turned to her mother and
said: "You don't know him — he's capable of
anything, even murder."

Daisy Letts naturally assumed this to be the typical
exaggeration of an angry woman.

Back at 25 Midland Road, in November 1971, the
Wests made the acquaintance of their next door
neighbour, Elizabeth Agius, a young mother with two
children, whose husband, a Maltese, worked abroad.
West saw her struggling with a pram, and offered to
help. They soon became acquainted, and Liz Agius
began to drop in regularly for tea with the Wests. Rose
seemed to her very young — she thought she looked
about fourteen. She agreed to baby-sit for them, and
on the second occasion, when they came back in the
early hours of the morning, she asked if they had
"been anywhere nice". Fred West replied: "We've
only been driving around looking for young girls." It
seems that West had ideas of solving his financial
problems by becoming a pimp. He said he wanted to
pick up girls of 16 or 17, runaways who would be glad
to find some kind of a home. It was possible, West
told her, to get far more money for a virgin. He took
Rose with him because girls trusted a couple more
than a single man. Asked later in court why she had
continued to be friendly with the Wests after such a
shocking conversation, she replied that she did not
believe it. "They were such a nice couple."

One day in the kitchen, Rose told Liz that her
husband was in love with her, and wanted to have
three-in-a-bed sex. Liz claims that she refused

indignantly. Rose also confided that she worked as a prostitute, and that Fred liked to watch through a hole in the wall. If Fred was not at home, she had to describe the sex in detail when he got home.

West soon became intensely possessive about Liz Agius, making it clear that he wanted to sleep with her. When her husband came on a visit, he was introduced to the Wests, and put his arm affectionately around his wife. Fred's reaction was violent jealousy — he leapt to his feet and rushed to the kitchen. Liz followed him to see what was the matter, and Rose followed soon after, to find Fred in a rage about Liz's husband, telling her that he ought to be "six feet under the ground." Then he produced a pair of handcuffs and snapped them on her wrists, saying: "Now I've fucking got you." Rose quickly released her.

This strange episode makes it clear that where sex was concerned West was incapable of rational behaviour. He wanted Liz Agius, and was totally unable to accept that her husband had a prior claim. Emotionally, Fred West was still a spoilt child.

On Liz Agius's next visit, Fred continued his strange wooing. He told her that he would like to tie her up and "do things to her", and that he would like her to tie him to the bed and whip him or burn him. And Rose seemed perfectly willing to allow this to happen.

Liz Agius took this to be a sign of their total trust in one another. But next time she dropped in for tea, she learned the truth. She was given her usual cup of tea, but this one made her feel dizzy. She woke up to find herself naked in bed between an equally naked Fred and Rose. Fred admitted that he had made love to her while she was unconscious.

Liz Agius allowed the Wests to dress her, and to

take her — and her baby — back home. It must have been a strong dose of the drug, for she still felt strange the next day.

Oddly enough, she seemed to feel no resentment about being raped, and continued to be friendly with the Wests.

In court in 1995, she would deny the story about the drugged tea, screaming: "I have never been in bed with the Wests." The prosecution went on to suggest that when Rose West had returned from having Mae in hospital in June 1972, she had found her husband in Liz Agius's flat, in bed with Fred, and had to beat on the bedroom door with her fists. Liz Agius denied this. But the following day in court, it was revealed that she had told the police about the tea-drugging episode, and also warned that she would deny it in court because of its possible consequences for her marriage.

Her friendship with the Wests continued; when they moved into Cromwell Street, she went to see them, and was taken over the house. She also recalled being taken down into the cellar through a trapdoor, which was not built until 1975; so it is clear that the friendship continued for a long time.

On January 29, 1972, Fred and Rose had finally married at the Gloucester Registry Office, where West described himself as a bachelor. Rose told Mae how Fred was repairing an old car to within half an hour of the wedding and had to be persuaded to change out of his overalls. His brother John witnessed the marriage, and another friend who had so many aliases he had to scribble out the first name he wrote on the certificate. On the way back, Fred found some money in the park which covered the cost of the marriage licence. I remember he was over the moon.

Stephen was to comment that his father always

walked around staring into the gutter, and that he proved remarkably lucky at finding money.

"We had no honeymoon," said Rose. "We just went to the Wellington pub and he bought one drink. He asked me what I wanted and I said a lager and lime. He said 'You have a bloody Coke and like it.'"

But according to Howard Sounes, Fred and Rose went off on a brief honeymoon to Devon. Rita New, the former neighbour of the Letts family, saw them in the Golden Lion public house in Northam, and was introduced to Fred — and to a blonde young woman who seemed to be accompanying them on their honeymoon, and who was referred to as a "girlfriend of Fred's." Fred and Rose were gesticulating so much that Rita New thought they might be high on drugs, but it seems more likely that neither of them was used to alcohol — it was only in later years, when Rose turned "professional", that they could afford to drink. The identity of the — presumably bisexual — girlfriend has never been established.

Back in Midland Road, a new problem was looming on the horizon in the person of Rena West, who wanted to keep in touch with Charmaine and Rose. Some time in August 1972, she called at Fred's old home Moorcourt Cottage, and was told that Fred's father was working on the harvest down at Moorcourt Farm. She went off looking for him, and returned some hours later; she had been helping with the harvest, and took a bath.

Her only possible motive for wanting to speak to Fred's father — now a widower — could have been a desire to find out about her children.

Clearly, the Wests were in trouble — immediate and urgent trouble. It was fortunate that Fred had not told his family the tale he had told Charmaine's school — that she had gone to London with her mother. If Rena demanded access to Charmaine, they would probably receive a visit from the social services. And inability to explain their daughter's whereabouts would certainly lead to a police investigation.

That seems to be the reason that, some time in the late summer of 1972, Rena disappeared. In the year following the discovery of the bodies at Cromwell Street, newspapers seemed to take it for granted that Rena West was murdered on New Year's Day 1969. In fact, there seems little doubt that she was killed between mid-August and early September 1972 — probably mid-August, since the Wests had an important reason for wanting to silence her after she had been to Moorcourt Cottage.

In his "confession", Fred was to describe how he took her out to a pub, got her drunk, then strangled her. He also claimed that Charmaine was asleep in the back of the car at the time, and that he also had to strangle Charmaine to prevent her from finding out.

This does not make even minimal sense. Would a couple take an eight-year-old child out with them when they were going for a drink — in the days when children were not permitted in English pubs? And what, in any case, was to prevent Fred West from taking the sleeping child back and allowing her to assume that her mother had simply gone home? It is clear that this whole story about killing Charmaine after he had killed Rena was simply an attempt to provide Rose with an alibi — an alibi that collapsed in court because Shirley Giles remembered that Charmaine had disappeared while Fred was in prison.

The truth is almost certainly that Rena was pounced upon when she came to Midland Road to enquire about Charmaine, punched or throttled unconscious, and carried down to the cellar. It would be natural to assume that West would want to kill and dispose of his wife as quickly as possible, but there is one disturbing piece of evidence that indicates otherwise. When her remains were found in Letter Box Field on June 7, 1994, a piece of chromium tubing found in the grave suggests that she might have been kept alive, with a mask of tape over her face (although no tape was found.) The body had not merely been dismembered; her left kneecap, and a number of bones of fingers and toes were missing. It looks as if, once he had his wife in his power, West indulged his usual morbid sexual abnormalities — including mutilation. Rena had declined to take part in his perversions during their marriage; now he could take his revenge after death.

Oddly enough, a red toy boomerang was also found in the grave, which Brian Masters, in *She Must Have Known*, cites as evidence of Rose's innocence — suggesting that Charmaine was present that night. Sounes is probably closer to the truth when he suggests that it was used to abuse her body. A less sinister alternative is that it simply found its way into the plastic bags in which West placed the body parts. (The basement was the children's playroom.)

West once again drove out to the place where he had buried Ann McFall. This time he chose Letter Box Field, immediately adjoining Fingerpost Field, and selected a spot under the hedgerow near the coppice. He dug the same kind of five-foot hole that he had dug for Ann McFall, threw in the bags, and covered them up. As he drove back to Gloucester in the dawn, he must have sighed with relief that a difficult and dangerous problem had been solved.

6
SEX GAMES

Our problem is to try to understand how two human beings, in many ways normal and well adjusted, could allow such a psychological gulf to open up between themselves and the rest of the human race. To call them monsters simply fails to get to grips with the problem. Even to compare Rose to a Nazi concentration camp guard is misleading, because Belsen and Auschwitz were restricted environments in which ruthlessness towards prisoners had become a matter of habit, while 25 Cromwell Street was in many ways a normal household, revolving around shopping, cooking and sending the children off to school.

What we have to grasp is that the relationship between two sexually obsessed people creates abnormal conditions — like the warm, damp conditions under which bio-organisms are cultured on gelatine in the laboratory.

Such conditions did not even begin to exist in western society until the second half of the 19th century. Sex crime, in our modern sense — as an expression of sexual fantasy, rather than mere opportunistic rape — was virtually non-existent before that. The reason is that life for the majority was incredibly hard. Many shops opened as a matter of course at 5 a.m, and stayed open until the late evening. Labourers worked for fourteen hours a day, for a wage barely enough to support a family. In most major cities, one flourishing trade was walking around with a bucket collecting dog manure, which was then sold to tanneries. Under such conditions, people were too busy staying alive to fantasise about sex. Only the wealthy had the necessary leisure, which is why the few recorded examples of sex crime in earlier centuries concern members of the upper classes like Gilles de Rais, Countess Elizabeth Bathory and the Marquis de Sade.

Even Sade, whose name is associated with cruelty, never actually murdered anyone — his worst crime was almost killing two prostitutes with an aphrodisiac. But Sade spent his years in prison — in the late 18th century — writing violent, anti-authoritarian novels in which rage and frustration find expression in descriptions of rape and murder. In effect, Sade started the European pornography industry, and by 1830 Amsterdam had become the major exporter of books about the seduction of children and the violation of virgins.

Sooner or later, all this fantasy was bound to find expression in reality. An English clerk called Frederick Baker, and two Americans, a youth named Jesse Pomeroy and a churchwarden named Thomas Piper, have the dubious distinction of being the earliest recorded sex killers. But the Jack the Ripper murders in London's East End in 1888 made the world aware that a new type of crime had arrived. Yet at the time most people failed to recognise the Ripper's five murders as sex killings; many thought he was a religious maniac protesting against prostitution. It could be said that Jack the Ripper inaugurated "the Age of Sex Crime", which has continued down to our own time.

The sex criminal is usually a loner, a man obsessed by his own fantasies. A typical example is William Heirens, a University of Chicago student, who began to commit burglaries at the age of twelve to obtain women's panties, with which he masturbated. Soon he began to experience orgasm climbing through windows. If interupted during the burglary, his sexual tension exploded into violence. In June 1945, when he was 17, he stabbed to death a woman named Josephine Ross, and in October 1945, fractured a woman's skull with an iron bar and tied her to a chair. Two months later, ex-Wave Frances Brown was found murdered and mutilated in bed; over her head the killer had scrawled: "For heavens sake catch me before I kill more. I cannot control myself." In January 1946, he carried a sleeping child, six-year-old Suzanne Degnan, out of her apartment, strangled her, then dismembered the body.

Caught when burgling an apartment in June 1946, Heirens finally confessed to the murders. He described how he had fought against the urge to commit burglary, but how, if he resisted it too long, he began to experience blinding headaches. On one occasion he had locked his clothes in the bathroom and thrown the key inside; but halfway through the night, had experienced such an overwhelming compulsion that he had crawled along the gutter to retrieve them, and went out. He mentioned that when he was looking for an apartment to burgle, it made no difference if he was lightly clad and the weather was freezing; "I could not feel any temperature." (The necrophile Sergeant Bertrand had swum an icy pond in midwinter to reach a graveyard.) Heirens was sentenced to life imprisonment.

This is "sex mania" into its simplest form; a young

and inexperienced person (Heirens was a virgin) for whom the very thought of sex creates a kind of fever. None of the victims was raped — Heirens had by then begun to associate sex with underwear and with the "forbidden" act of burglary, so that burglary itself created the sexual tension.

Until recent years, most sex criminals fell into this category of the "obsessive loner." Until fairly recent decades, there were virtually no examples involving "killer couples." One of the few exceptions was the case of Nathan Leopold and Richard Loeb in 1924. The two University of Chicago students were sons of wealthy families, and formed a criminal alliance, committing burglaries "for kicks." Both were interested in the philosophy of Nietzsche, and decided to commit a murder to prove that they were Nietzschean "supermen". They chose 14-year-old Bobbie Franks, the son of a local businessman, and beat him to death after offering him a ride in their car. Leopold was identified by his glasses, left near the body, and both were sentenced to life imprisonment.

In the characters of the two killers we can see the pattern typical of such crimes. Richard Loeb was the dominant one: handsome, extraverted, charming; Nathan Leopold was shy and studious. He fell in love with Loeb, and Loeb became his lover on condition that he participated in burglaries. Their first intention was to kill and rape a girl (both were bisexual), but they abandoned this in favour of a kidnap that might bring a large ransom. Leopold wrote letters to Loeb addressing him as "Master", and signing himself "Slave."

Here, as in the Heirens case, sex and crime have become so closely associated that crime brings a sexual thrill. But, as in the Heirens case, there was no rape involved.

One of the first cases of a married couple involved in sex crime took place in 1963 in Lansing, Michigan, when 24-year-old Lloyd Higdon and his wife offered a lift to a 14-year-old neighbour, who was taken to their home and ordered to undress, after which Higdon had sex with her. He was charged with statutory rape (sex with an underage girl), since she had made no resistance, and sent to prison. Released two years later, Higdon and a girlfriend named Lucille Brumit picked up a 13-year-old girl and drove her to a rubbish dump. When she resisted rape, Higdon strangled her. Picked up as a known sex offender, he eventually confessed, and was sentenced to life imprisonment.

It is not known whether any lesbian element was involved in the assaults; all that is certain is that Higdon was able to dominate two women to the extent of helping him commit rape.

In England at the same time, Ian Brady and Myra Hindley, the "Moors Murderers", killed at least five children and young people, in a pact that recalls Leopold and Loeb. Brady was a social rebel, who had been in trouble for burglary since the age of 13. Infuriated by a two-year Borstal sentence for aiding and abetting a lorry driver to load stolen goods, Brady vowed revenge on society. He planned to get rich on armed robbery, and retire to South America.

In Manchester, working for a small chemical firm, Brady met 18-year-old Myra Hindley, nearly five years his junior. In Abraham Maslow's terms, she was definitely "medium dominance", a romantic young girl who had had a religious upbringing, and who looked forward to marriage and a family. She fell hopelessly in love with the high-dominance Brady, who ignored her for nearly a year before finally inviting her out, and taking her virginity on a settee.

He quickly converted her to atheism and Nazism, and to the philosophy of de Sade. As in the Leopold and Loeb case, he was the Master, she the Slave. His major satisfaction undoubtedly derived from his sense of dominating her. She took a little persuading to join him in the planned robbery of a bank or building society. But in July 1963 she agreed to help him in the rape and murder of a neighbour, 16-year-old Pauline Reade. She was lured for a ride to the moors in Myra's minivan; then Brady arrived on his motorbike, and raped her, finally cutting her throat. She was buried on the moor.

The next victim was a 12-year-old boy, John Kilbride, who was offered a lift by Myra, and murdered and probably raped by Brady (who was bisexual) in November 1963. In June 1964, 12-year-old Keith Bennett was abducted and killed. In December 1964 the victim was 10-year-old Lesley Ann Downey, who was taken back to the house they shared with Myra's grandmother; her cries for mercy were recorded on tape. Like the other victims, she was buried on the moors.

Brady then made the mistake of trying to involve Myra's brother-in-law, David Smith, in his crimes. He and Myra invited a 17-year-old homosexual, Edward Evans, back to the house, and Brady battered him to death in front of Smith. Smith was so shocked that he told his wife, and she persuaded him to call the police. The body was still in the house when police arrived the next day and arrested Brady and Myra Hindley. Both pleaded Not Guilty, but were sentenced to life imprisonment. They have since confessed to the murders.

Here there can be no doubt that Brady shaped Myra to his own image. He was to allege later that she had also sexually assaulted Pauline Reade, and strangled Lesley Ann Downey, and he may well be telling the truth; like Nathan Leopold, Myra was totally besotted. What seems abundantly clear is that Myra Hindley would never have become a killer unless she had met Ian Brady. The Moors Murders can only be understood in terms of Brady's dominance, and the pleasure he took in exercising it. It may be said — although with no attempt to excuse her — that she was literally brainwashed.

California, in the late 1970s, had its own equivalent of the Moors Murders. But it also bears some interesting resemblances to the West case. Charlene Williams was the daughter of a wealthy Sacramento businessman, and had been married and divorced twice by the age of 21; she had been indulging in drugs and sex since her early teens. In 1977, she met an ex-convict named Gerald Gallego on a blind date, and was enchanted by his dominance and his sexual virility. Gallego was the son of a man who had been executed for murder, and his life was dominated by a craving for sex and a hatred of authority. Like Fred West, he is believed to have had a sexual relationship with his mother, who in turn had been sexually abused by her father and grandfather. Like Brady, Gallego dreamed of revenge on society, telling a fellow-prisoner: "The only thing I want is to kill God."(Brady had once shook his fist at the sky after one of the murders, and shouted: "Take that, you bastard.")

Gallego also told Charlene that he dreamed of "the perfect sex slave", and during the next three years she collaborated with him on ten rape murders. They were finally arrested after kidnapping a young couple in November 1980; the man was killed, and the girl raped and then murdered. But a friend of the couple had taken the number of the car in which they were driven away, and Gallego and Charlene Williams were arrested after a tip-off from her parents.

Charlene insisted that she had been Gallego's "slave", and collaborated on the murders because he forced her to. The first book on the case, *All His Father's Sins*, by Ray Biondi and Walt Hecox, takes Charlene's view. But an investigator named Eric van Hoffmann told another story in *Venom in the Blood*. He claimed that Charlene was a bisexual nymphomaniac who had taken an active part in the sexual assaults. According to Hoffmann, Gallego had become impotent with Charlene after finding her engaged in lesbian sex. But on his daughter's fourteenth birthday, when Gallego had sex with both her and her girlfriend, Charlene realised that Gallego was far from impotent, and suggested the idea of kidnapping and murdering girls. (Gallego had first seduced his daughter when she was six.) She helped him abduct girls — sometimes in pairs — by luring them to the car on a promise of pot-smoking. Then, according to Hoffmann, Gallego and Charlene played an equal part in the rapes, Charlene forcing the girls to perform oral sex on her. On one occasion, Charlene almost bit off a girl's nipple. Afterwards Gallego shot the girls, or battered them to death.

One victim, a waitress named Virginia Mochel, whom they abducted and then spent the night violating, had found it so degrading that she begged them to kill her.

Charlene Williams turned State's Evidence, and was sentenced to sixteen years; Gallego was sentenced to die by lethal injection.

There is another case of duo-murder that offers even more crucial insights into the West case. It was tried in Toronto, Canada, a few months before the trial of Rose West, and the defendant was Paul Bernardo, a handsome young businessman in his late twenties, who resembled President Bill Clinton; his girlfriend and accomplice, Karla Homolka, a dazzling blonde, six years his junior, had been tried and sentenced earlier. They were accused of two murders of teenage girls, Leslie Mahaffy and Kristen French, and of the death by drugging of Karla's teenage sister Tammy.

Karla Homolka had been 17-years-old when she met Paul Bernardo in the dining room of a Howard Johnson's hotel in Scarborough, a suburb of Toronto; she and a girlfriend had booked in for the night. The girls had invited Paul Bernardo and his friend Van Smirnis to their room, and within minutes Bernardo and Karla were in bed, having wild and orgiastic sex; Smirnis and the girlfriend, on the other bed, watched them with a certain envy. It was obvious that Bernardo and Karla had some extraordinary chemical affinity. Later, it became clear that this affinity was based upon the fact that his sexual tastes veered towards sadism, and hers towards masochism. At 16, Karla had allowed a boyfriend to tie her up with his belt and slap her during sex, and discovered that she enjoyed it. The first time she and Paul were alone in her bedroom, he found handcuffs in her pocket, and asked: "Are these for me?" Then he handcuffed her to the bed and they pretended he was raping her. As their relationship progressed, she had to pretend to be a schoolgirl — with her hair in pigtails tied with ribbons — while he was a successful businessman returning exhausted from the office, to be sexually stimulated by the adoring schoolgirl; their game included handcuffs and a dog chain. He liked her to wear a dog collar round her neck when they had sex. He also liked her to perform fellatio and anilingus, and he liked to sodomise her.

When she met Paul Bernardo, Karla was unaware that he was the man the police referred to as the Scarborough Rapist. Since May that year, the rapist had been grabbing women who alighted from buses. He liked to rape the victims vaginally and anally; he also liked to humiliate them calling them names like cunt, slut, whore, and to force them to tell him that he was the best lover they had ever had. Often he pounded them with his fists as he raped them. These attacks continued for years after Bernardo met Karla Homolka.

Some time before Christmas 1990, Karla had asked Bernardo — by now engaged to her, and living in her home — what he wanted for Christmas, and Bernardo had replied: "Your sister Tammy." Tammy was 15, and still at school. During sex sessions Karla had to answer to the name "Tam" and pretend to be her sister. Bernardo had been pressing Karla for some time to help him rape Tammy, but she had refused; now, finally, she gave way. She obtained drugs from the animal clinic where she worked, and on the evening of December 23, 1990, they invited Tammy to join them in watching a film after midnight in the basment "den", and gave her drugged drinks. When she was unconscious, Bernardo undressed her and raped her on the floor, then sodomised her. While Bernardo worked the video camera, he made Karla perform oral sex on her sister.

It was while Bernardo was having more vaginal and anal sex with Tammy — filmed by Karla — that he noticed that the girl had stopped breathing, and her face had turned blue. Tammy died in hospital, but no suspicion fell on her sister or Bernardo; the inquest seemed to show that she had drunk too much, and choked on her own vomit.

Bernardo and Karla began to play a game in which he stared at a picture of Tammy, and Karla pretended to be Tammy as Bernardo took her virginity. If Karla occasionally protested about these fantasy sessions, and the indignities to which she was subjected, Bernardo beat her. Her close friends began to note that she was often covered in bruises; Karla always found some excuse to explain them.

On Friday, June 14, 1991, a 14-year-old schoolgirl named Leslie Mahaffy arrived home at 2.am to find herself locked out. Bernardo found her sitting disconsolately on a bench in her backyard, and offered her a cigarette. Then he held a knife to her throat, forced her to lie down in his car, and blindfolded her. He took her back to the house that he and Karla now shared — they were due to get married in two weeks — then made her undress. He videotaped her urinating on the toilet, then raped her vaginally and anally, and made her perform oral sex on him.

He woke Karla to tell her that he had kidnapped a girl, but told her to go back to sleep. But the next day she had to join in, having lesbian sex with the schoolgirl while Bernardo videotaped them. Leslie was also raped repeatedly. When left alone with Karla, the schoolgirl begged her to let her go; Karla replied that if she did, she would be beaten. She gave Leslie two sleeping tablets to "make her feel better", and while Leslie was asleep, Bernardo looped electrical cord around her throat and strangled her.

Two days later, he sawed up the body with an electric saw, encased the pieces in quick-drying cement, then dropped them off a bridge into Lake Gibson, with Karla acting as lookout.

Bernardo now decided to seduce a 15-year-old schoolgirl named Jane, who had been a friend of

Tammy's. Jane was invited to the house of the newly-weds, was flattered by the attention of two adults, and developed a schoolgirl crush on Karla. One night, she was given drugged liquor, and after she fell asleep Karla anaesthetised her with halothane, obtained from the animal clinic. Bernardo then raped and sodomised her while Karla videoed it; Bernardo was particularly delighted to find that Jane had been a virgin.

Suddenly Jane stopped breathing, and there were five minutes of panic as they telephoned an ambulance. Then she began breathing again, and they cancelled the ambulance. She woke up in their house the next day without even suspecting what had happened.

But it was not enough to have possessed her; Bernardo wanted her to give herself to him willingly. Jane resisted, feeling it would be a betrayal of Karla — even Karla's assurance that she would not mind made no difference. But Bernardo often took Jane to a bedroom on the pretext of talking to her, and persuaded her to perform oral sex. Although she continued to refuse to allow him to make love to her, she finally performed oral sex on demand. It was not until the videotape was shown in court that Jane would realise that she had also been raped.

On April 6, 1992, ten months after the murder of Leslie Mahaffy, Karla accompanied Bernardo as they drove in search of another victim. They passed fifteen-year-old Kristen French, walking alone on her way home from school, and Karla called to ask her instructions. The girl came over to their car as Karla produced a map. Then Bernardo moved behind her and forced her into the car at knifepoint.

Back in their house, Bernardo made the girl crouch on the floor like an animal while he raped her vaginally and anally; when she refused to fellate him, he punched her until she gave way. After that, Karla brought drinks on a silver tray. When Kristen wanted to go to the lavatory, Bernardo filmed her. Later, Karla had to film Kristen performing oral sex on Bernardo, before which she was forced to say: "I am fifteen and I love to suck dick." Then Karla performed oral sex on Kristen, and Bernardo raped her again.

After three days more of rape, and being forced to take part in videotapes in which she had to address him as "master", Kristen, like Leslie Mahaffy, was murdered. Her naked body was thrown on a dumpsite full of old washing machines.

During the New Year, 1993, Bernardo beat Karla more violently than usual, clubbing her with a rubber flashlight and blacking both her eyes. Finally, her mother and sister called when Bernardo was out, and insisted on taking her to hospital. After that she agreed to go home with them. To prevent her husband discovering her whereabouts, she moved in with an aunt and uncle.

In late January of 1993, after six years, the Toronto police finally solved the Scarborough rapist case. There had been 224 suspects, among these Paul Bernardo, who resembled an identikit drawing of the rapist. Bernardo had given a body sample to be compared with the sperm of the rapist, but had heard nothing further in two years, and assumed he was clear. In fact, the DNA testing had proceeded with incredible slowness, and Bernardo was among the last five suspects whose body sample was tested. It was only then that the police knew that Paul Bernardo was the Scarborough rapist.

Instead of arresting him immediately, the police went to interview Karla Homolka. She refused to tell them anything, but when they had gone, blurted out to her uncle and aunt: "Christ, they know everything." Pressed by her aunt, Karla finally told her about the murder of the two schoolgirls.

Bernardo was arrested on February 17, 1993. Karla Homolka turned State's Evidence against her husband, in what is known in legal slang as a "sweetheart deal" — that is, in exchange for a promise of a lighter sentence. She was tried first, and was sentenced to twelve years.

The police had not been able to find the videotapes of the prolonged sexual ordeals of Leslie Mahaffy and Kristen French. But they finally discovered that Bernardo's lawyer had them, and they were at last handed over to the authorities. Bernardo's trial opened on May 1, 1995. It was as sensational as everyone had expected, with videotapes showing the rapes, and of Karla performing fellatio while Bernardo rubs Tammy's panties against his penis; she tells him that she feels proud of him for the death of her sister.

On September 1, 1995, Paul Bernardo was sentenced to life imprisonment, with the proviso that he should serve a minimum of 25 years before he could apply for parole.

What emerges very clearly from the two books that have so far been published about the case is that Paul Bernardo wanted to play games of "let's pretend", like a child. After Karla tells him that it is her mission in life to make him feel good, Bernardo holds up his lager to the camera and says: "Skol to the king." During the final session with Kristen French, shortly before he strangles her, he makes her say things like: "You're my master and my boyfriend. You're the king. You're the most powerful man in the world. All the girls in my school want to fuck you because you're the most powerful man in the world." And while he is listening to this and raping her, Bernardo turns to his wife and says: "Lick my ass, bitch." But as he climaxes, ordering his wife to get him a box of tissues, Kristen says defiantly: "I don't know how your wife can stand being around you." A few moments later, with the camera off, he strangled her.

The scene offers us a glimpse into the basic motivation of sex crime. From the beginning, Bernardo had been a fantasist, feeding his obsession with pornographic videos. He graduated to being a Peeping Tom, masturbating as he watched girls undressing. By comparison with this fantasy sex, real sex — which he always found easy to obtain — was anticlimactic.

When he was 19, Bernardo seduced a 16-year-old high-school girl. Since she was totally inexperienced, she was unaware that some of his sexual demands — like fellatio and anal intercourse — were abnormal. But on one of the last occasions they went out together, he drove to an empty parking lot and snapped: "Get in the back seat, bitch." When she was undressed, he picked up a wine bottle, and told her: "Stick that up your cunt." As she did this he ordered her to get on her knees, and tied her hands behind her. "Get your ass in the air." He tied another piece of twine around her neck, and pulled it tight as he sodomised her, telling her: "I'm the king and you're the servant girl." Finally he climaxed, telling her afterwards: "You were great tonight."

Next time they had sex he was even rougher, and she finally stopped seeing him.

Mere lovemaking bored him. He greatly preferred sodomy, because it was more of a "surrender." When he began committing rapes in 1987, he would force his victims to repeat things like "I'm a cunt",

"I'm a cocksucker", or to assure him that they loved him.

What Bernardo was doing, in effect, was dramatising a pornographic fantasy. Pornography was more exciting than normal sex, but if normal sex could be turned into pornography, then he was getting the best of both worlds. Like Gallego, he was looking for the "perfect sex slave", or rather, the perfect fantasy.

But all sexual fantasy is addictive, and, like a drug, needs to be taken in larger doses. The purpose of a drug is to blot out the real world, to enable the drug-taker to retreat into a private reality, like an opium addict, or a child listening to a fairy story. Bernardo's step from Peeping Tom to rapist was a sign of his need for increasing doses.

But the meeting with Karla was crucial. And it also enables us to understand something about the relation between Fred and Rose West. Karla was undoubtedly one of Maslow's dominant women. As a child she occasionally shocked the neighbourhood by shouting: "Fuck off!" She was, says her best friend Lisa, an obsessive talker, and "stubborn and wilful." She was unwilling to admit that she might be wrong, and would never back down, even when an argument was clearly lost. In short, she is virtually a female equivalent of Van Vogt's "Right Man."

Now, in his studies in dominance in women Abraham Maslow made an interesting observation. Both dominant males and females were interested only in sex partners within their own dominance group. High-dominance males might seduce medium or low-dominance females, but there was no real personal interest. To get personally involved, the male needed a woman within his own dominance group. Dominant women were not interested in medium or low dominance men; they needed a male who belonged to the "dominant 5%."

Yet Maslow also discovered that all women — whether of high, medium or low dominance — preferred a male who was slightly more dominant than themselves. He describes one case of a woman who was so highly dominant that she never succeeded in finding a male of greater dominance. Finally, she met a man whose dominance was roughly equal to her own. But she only found sex with him truly satisfying if she could provoke him into a rage in which he hurled her on the bed and virtually raped her. Here we see, as in Karla Homolka, that a high-dominance woman can nevertheless be masochistic.

Since the dominant 5% consists of only one person in twenty, Karla Homolka's chance of finding a more dominant male were obviously less than that — since most dominant males would be less dominant than herself. A single glance at Paul Bernardo told her instinctively that he was what she had been looking for. She had had only one boyfriend, to whom she lost her virginity, but he was clearly not dominant enough. Bernardo was, which is why she was in bed with him within an hour of meeting him.

Van Smirnis decribes how, as he and Karla's girlfriend lay on the other bed, the bedsheets on Bernardo's bed erupted into activity. When the sheet fell off, Karla could be seen sitting astride Bernardo, her hips grinding. Then Bernardo pulled Karla down underneath him. "It was as if the two were fighting for who would be on top, who would dominate the other." And clearly, it was Bernardo who won. Karla had found her dominant male. From then on, he was the most important thing in her life. He was handsome, ambitious, succcessful (at that time he was a junior accountant at Price Waterhouse) —

everything she had ever wanted.

For Bernardo, on the other hand, Karla was merely another woman. It was true that she belonged to his own dominance group; but his sexual fantasy was a desire to possess all women; he was the king, the sultan, and all women were his harem. He was not particularly anxious to form a close personal relationship; what he wanted was a "slave" — or preferably a dozen or so.

This realisation brought out all Karla's latent masochism. And the relationship that proceeded to develop was basically very similar to that between Ian Brady and Myra Hindley. Part of Bernardo's pleasure came from the fact that Karla was dominant, but that she still accepted him as her "king." He was allowed relationships with other women, but she was not allowed relationships with other men (one of the typical characteristics of the Right Man). Karla decribed how she and Bernardo "would often go across the border to the Pleasure Dome and he would go off and meet other girls and dance, while she was allowed to dance only when Paul wanted her to. Otherwise she had to sit where Paul positioned her and not complain." And while they were living at her parents' home, he went out telling her he meant to pick up a girl, and that if she met the girl she was to pretend to be his sister. Karla hid behind a curtain in the basement and watched as Bernardo spent two hours having sex with a sixteen-year-old.

Karla undoubtedly had a streak of masochism, but this is perhaps less important than the fact that she felt she had found her Mr Right, and was willing to put up with a great deal to keep him. To begin with, she accepted his sadism as an expression of his sexuality, and participated enthusiastically in his games of make-believe, even when it involved her sleeping in a cold basement with no covering. (Like Rose West, Bernardo had an uncontrollable temper, and felt no inhibition about exploding into screaming violence.) She believed his assertion that he would end as a millionaire, and was determined to make their marriage a success.

But as it slowly became clear that his violence was partly an expression of contempt for her as a person, her infatuation began to wear off. When she forgot to video a TV programme, he made her write a hundred times: "I must never forget to record The Simpsons." Finally, she came to accept beatings as a matter of course. He even forced her to eat his excrement as a punishment, although he finally allowed her to wrap it in paper before she swallowed it.

The final beating was due to her reluctance to help him kidnap and rape yet another girl; this time, he wanted her to do the killing. He usually beat her on the body; this time he hit her in the face.

Even so, she had no thought of leaving him until her mother and sister virtually kidnapped her and took her to the hospital. Only then did she realise how relieved she felt to be free again.

Bernardo emerges from the trial evidence as the ultimate Right Man — his whole life was a non-stop game in which he was the Man of Power, the King, the Great Mogul. There was no actual sadism in his relationships with his kidnap victims; he did not beat them with a belt or whip them, as Fred West did. He was simply carrying sexual fantasy to its ultimate, treating a real person as if she was a figment of his imagination.

When Karla left Bernardo, he was shattered, as Right Men always are under such circumstances. The reason should be clear. His home had become a kind of Aladdin's cave; when he walked through his front door, he was no longer in the harsh real world, but in a kind of Arabian Nights fantasy, in which he was Haroun Al Raschid. His wife literally bowed at his feet and called him master. On the orders of her master, she produced drugs and helped him to deflower virgins. He kidnapped schoolgirls, she participated in their rape. And the schoolgirls too were made to acknowledge him as their master, and assure him that every girl in their school would like to be deflowered by him. And when he grew tired of them, he would strangle them and discard them. In his own home he was master of the world, the Lord of Reality.

Now, suddenly, his Aladdin's cave had collapsed around him, and the cold wind of reality was blowing in. He made a tape for Karla in which he told her he was about to commit suicide, and which showed remarkable insight into himself. "Here's the problem, Kar. I tried to be larger than life. I really did. I didn't want to be average, like the average guy. I tried to be larger, the best thing that there ever was."

There was a sense in which he probably did not even feel guilty. He had not committed real crimes, but crimes of the imagination. As far as he was concerned, the only thing of which he could justifiably be accused was of trying to force reality to conform to his imagination — like every great man in the history of the world ...

It is this insight that offers the key to all cases of duo-murder, *folie à deux*. Leopold and Loeb were playing a game of supermen, in which they were allowed to transgress all the laws of society; crime was an essential part of this game, because it brought a thrill that was akin to sex. (Bernardo was also a lifelong crook, engaging in various "scams", and at the time of his arrest, had given up his job with Price Waterhouse to make a living smuggling cigarettes across the Canadian border.) Ian Brady and Myra Hindley played the same game, planning robberies which never took place, but indulging in child-murder.

Gerald Gallego and Charlene Williams had no need to play games about crime because Gallego was already a convict with many convictions for robbery. But their relationship was also based on "game-playing." For Gallego, she was the wealthy girl who amplified his self-esteem by surrendering to him; for Charlene, he was the dangerous criminal who could make her feel as if she was eating dinner with a tiger. He was also, according to many women, a lover of formidable prowess. But Charlene spoiled the game by having lesbian sex, thereby striking at the foundation of his self-esteem, his feeling that he gave the orders.

Significantly, his daughter Mary Ellen also spoiled the sex game he had been playing since she was six. For Gallego she was the perfect mistress because she adored him and regarded him as a kind of god. She was intensely jealous of his relation with Charlene. (Charlene liked to call Gallego "daddy" because she knew it sexually excited him.) But when, on her fourteenth birthday, she came to see her father with a companion of her own age, Gallego sodomised his daughter, and persuaded her companion to fellate him. Charlene joined in.

The experience seems to have turned Mary Ellen against him. Until then she had felt she had a special relation with her father, his daughter-wife. But with two other women joining in, it must suddenly have dawned on her that she had never been anything more than a victim of a father with an omnivorous sexual appetite.

It was after this that Mary Ellen decided to tell her grandfather — who had brought her up — about the eight years of incest. He almost went insane, and when Gallego came back from a store, was waiting with a deer rifle. Gallego's mother succeeded in locking him in a bedroom while her son escaped, but her husband rang the police. Gallego became once more a fugitive from the law.

And so another sex game collapsed. Now they had to invent another game that allowed Charlene to express her lesbian tendencies and Gallego to play the criminal — this time the killer. Not long after this, Charlene accosted two teenage girls in a shopping mall in Sacramento, lured them to the Oldsmobile with a promise of marihuana, then joined in as both were raped on a mattress in the back. Then they drove them to a lonely spot, and Gallego killed them both. And so the games went on for another two years — and eight victims — until they were caught.

All this enables us to begin to understand the relation between Fred and Rose West. Like Bernardo, he boasted of his business success, and like Gallego, he was a crook; the fifteen-year-old Rose was easily impressed. But Rose herself — like Karla Homolka and Charlene Williams — was herself a person of high dominance, and this is what cemented the relationship between herself and Fred, and made them ultimately inseparable. (The little we know of Rena and Ann McFall suggests they were women of medium dominance.)

We do not know as much about Fred West's sex life as we know about Bernardo's or Gallego's, but we know that he liked "domination." He liked to tie women up and flog them, which tells us that he liked to see himself as "the king." (He made Rose write him a note promising total obedience.) He also liked to make love to corpses, and to cut off fingers and toes — in that sense he was more perverted than Gallego, Bernardo or Brady. They killed their victims simply to dispose of them; West killed them as part of the sex ritual.

Fred and Rose West became a hunting team, like Gallego and Charlene Williams, or Brady and Myra Hindley. But she steadily became the more dominant of the two. It was she who decided that they "must get" Caroline Raine, and almost certainly she who decided that they had to "get" Lynda Gough and the other victims. And in the sex games that took place, her part was as dominant as that of Charlene Williams. Fred himself, as he later explained, was merely the undertaker.

The rapes and murders that followed were not, as far as the Wests were concerned, genuine crimes; they were simply part of a sex game that absorbed them more than anything else in their lives. We do not know the nature of their fantasies as they dragged in a kidnap victim and undressed her; but we know that they had left the real world behind, and were living inside their own heads.

7
THE TORTURE CHAMBER

After two years in a ground-floor flat, Fred and Rose wanted a house to themselves; and in early September 1972, they moved to 25 Cromwell Street, which they rented from their landlord Frank Zygmunt. It was a semi-detached house with a Seventh Day Adventist church next door, only a few hundred yards from their previous flat.

Like Midland Road, Cromwell Street had once been a middle class area; now it was something of a slum. When Liz Agius called on them she was invited to move in with them and work as a prostitute. She said that Fred showed her the basement, and joked that it was his "torture chamber."

During that autumn West began converting the house into bedsits, lodgers moved in, and Caroline Raine was installed as an au pair. Then — as described earlier — Caroline was kidnapped and raped, and the Wests escaped prison because the magistrates thought he looked harmless. Then they embarked on a full-time career as sex killers.

Anne Marie comments: "We lived in a vacuum at Cromwell Street ... The house was protected by big iron gates ... " Fred immediately began enlarging and deepening the cellar, carting out tons of earth in a wheelbarrow. It was originally too low for an adult to stand upright, but by the time he had deepened the foundations it was possible for an adult to stand with his — or her — arms stretched towards the ceiling; holes drilled in two beams also meant that it was possible to hang someone from them.

The Wests lived in the lower part of the house — ground floor and cellar — and the lodgers in the upper part. They led virtually separate lives. But the Wests were not quite as isolated as the children; Fred and Rose began to go to the local pubs at night — Anne Marie says they preferred "the rough ones" — and to a local drinking club where there were many West Indians. Even so, Fred spent most of his spare time working at his home improvements — for example, turning the garage where Lynda Gough was buried into a bathroom.

Lynda was murdered on or about April 20, 1973, and for a month or so afterwards the Wests must have wondered whether they had got away with it. Lynda was the first person to be buried at 25 Cromwell Street, and if her family pressed hard enough, they might persuade the police to search the premises — Rose had made a mistake wearing Lynda's slippers when she answered the door, and leaving some of Lynda's clothes visible on the clothes-line. If June Gough had decided that there was no evidence that her daughter had left 25 Cromwell Street, it could well have been the end of the career of the Wests as sexual predators. But, as with the rape of Caroline Raine, their luck held. Fred was beginning to feel that they were invulnerable.

Male callers continued to come and go, and Fred continued to gain his greatest sexual satisfaction from watching Rose having sex with them, and then having sex with her as soon as they had left.

As a prostitute, she was unusual. Most prostitutes

feel that it is a boring job; Rose obviously enjoyed it. (Stephen West recollected: "When she had finished, she always used to be a lot more relaxed, happier and polite.") The *Sun* would later succeed in interviewing some of her regular customers of the 1980s. Market trader John Holmes commented: "She was bloody good. It was the best sex I have had in years. We used to do it in her four poster bed upstairs. I was much older than her, but I gave her a good seeing to." Another customer, Charlie Murphy, saw an advertisement for "Mandy", and telephoned. "She said it was £10 for everything. Rose was wearing a flimsy pink outfit fastened at the crotch. She was plump, with full breasts, and knew how to excite a man. That first time she undressed me slowly, then we had oral sex. I was there for three-quarters of an hour and loved every minute. It was impossible for human beings to copulate in more ways. She was brilliant. The best sex ever." Murphy went on seeing her once or twice a week for six months,

Rose's nymphomania left behind a string of satisfied clients.

Mae states that Rose became a full "professional" only when she — Mae — was about fourteen, which would be in 1986. But since Mae herself was raped by one of the male callers when she was ten, it is clear that Rose continued to have a stream of lovers. Fred forced many of these on her — Mae says that Fred bullied Rose into going to bed with one particular black man who disgusted her.

But it would be a mistake to think of Rose as a victim. She had never been the type, and as she grew older, she grew more dominant. She took out her foul temper on Anne Marie, whom she disliked because she felt she was a rival for her husband's love. "She was very jealous of his time and affection. A kindly word from dad was often followed by a thump from Rose." There seems little doubt that the rape of Anne Marie, which occurred that summer, was Rose's idea, although the regular sexual intercourse that followed her ninth birthday was undoubtedly Fred's.

The novelty of abusing Anne Marie provided them with a diversion during that summer of 1973. But sooner or later Rose would want a girl with whom she could play the part of the butch male. One night in November, as they drove around around looking for a victim, they saw fifteen-year-old Carol Anne Cooper, who was on her way back to the children's home where she lived.

Like so many of the Wests' victims, Carol was the child of a broken home. She liked to be called Caz, and had tattooed that name with a pen nib on her forearm. Her father, Colin Cooper, was in the RAF when she was born on April 10, 1958, but he and his wife Mary separated when Carol was three. Carol adored her mother, and lived with her until, six years later, Mary Cooper died during an asthmatic attack. Carol was shattered, and her world collapsed.

She went to live with her father, but it was never the same. Colin Cooper had remarried, and was working as an insurance salesman. But Carol disliked her stepmother Barbara, who said later: "She was a rebellious girl, and used to say that I wasn't her real mum." When this second marriage also failed, Carol was taken into care, and placed in the Pines Children's Home in Bilton Road, Worcester, where her room was plastered with photographs of her dream male, Elvis Presley. At least she had many relatives in the town, including her grandmother, Alice Tonks, who lived near the children's home, and with whom she spent weekends. One relative said that Alice Tonks spoiled Carol as if she was her daughter.

Still emotionally crippled by the death of her mother, Carol continued to be "difficult", and talked about her boredom, and how she intended to run away to London. But her social worker, Elspeth Keir, described her "a lovely, intelligent girl", who had had a difficult life with many problems. "But I remember she had a sparkle in her blue eyes that said one day she intended to put it all behind her and make good."

On the cold afternoon of Saturday, November 10, 1973, Carol had gone into Worcester to meet her boyfriend Andrew Jones. With a large group of friends they went to the Odeon cinema, then for fish and chips, then to a pub, where Carol drank a bitter orange. Carol and Andrew had a quarrel and Carol cried. But they made it up, and at 9 o'clock, Andrew took her to the bus stop and gave her 18 pence for her fare to the home of her grandmother. As the bus drew away, Andrew waved to her.

That evening, when Carol failed to arrive home, her grandmother spent hours making enquiries. Later, there was a police search. But most of the relatives assumed that she had carried out her threat to run away to London.

What had happened seems clear. Fred and Rose West had decided to drive north looking for a teenage girl — Worcester is 25 miles north of Gloucester. It is unlikely that she accepted a lift, since she had the bus-fare to her grandmother's; it is more likely that Fred stopped the car and Rose asked directions; then Carol was dragged inside.

When her body was found, twenty-one years later, she was wearing a mask of tape; this was probably bound around her face while she was still in the car. She was driven back to Cromwell Street, and Rose would open the gates so that Fred could drive in. In the backyard, she could be dragged out in the dark and taken to the cellar.

All that we can state with certainty about what followed is that it was Rose who took the lead. For, unlike Gerald Gallego or Paul Bernardo, West had not organised this abduction primarily for his own pleasure, but for that of his partner. It would be Rose who undressed her. If West was telling Stephen West the truth in prison, he watched, and helped Rose achieve satiation. His job was the "undertaker" — to strangle the victim, satisfy his own necrophilia on the corpse, then achieve his ultimate satisfaction by dismembering it. Many mutilation murderers are betrayed by the blood they leave behind, but West would be in no hurry. The body would have been dead a long time before he dismembered it, so there would be no spurting — only a slow oozing of blood, which could be caught in a bucket, and poured down the drain outside the bathroom.

What seems so incomprehensible is not how Fred West could murder a girl and then dismember her, since we know from Terry Crick — and from his own children — that he had a morbid interest in female anatomy. "He really wanted to get inside them." What seems baffling is how Rose could force a 15-year-old girl to join in lovemaking with the full knowledge that she was to be killed.

The accounts given by her own children provide the answer. Being married to Fred had made her hard and brutal, and she actually seemed to enjoy losing control. It was not a question of being goaded into fury; she loved being carried away by her emotions like a surfer on a wave. Losing her temper was closely related to the noisy sexual abandonment that could be heard all over the house.

Anne Marie says: "I remember taking a beating

because she had lost a tea towel. She was in the living room, going round in circles, yelling 'Tea towel, tea towel!' and I just didn't get it to her quickly enough. I got belted too for not stirring the gravy in the right way and not mashing the potatoes properly. Sometimes you felt the back of her hand, but if she wanted to give you a good going-over, she would grab the nearest weapon, so that she didn't hurt herself. I was hit across the head with a broom on more than one occasion, and I still have a small scar where she knifed my hand.

"It was as if she had mental blackouts, almost as if she didn't know she was doing it. When she had finished, she would look up and say: 'Your fucking fault. You should have done it properly'. On other occasions she wouldn't speak; she'd just carry on with what she was doing as if nothing had happened."

On another occasion, Rose ordered Anne Marie into her bedroom, made her undress, then made the child perform cunnilingus on her. Anne Marie describes how she sneaked to the bathroom afterwards to wash out her mouth with mouthwash — making sure Rose did not suspect what she was doing.

Anne Marie also wrote: "Rose would have made a wonderful concentration camp guard ... Torture, both mental and physical, would have been her forte. Nothing would have pleased Rose more than to send many to their deaths and to have unlimited scope to experiment on them ... "

When Rose wanted something, nothing else mattered. She had none of the normal inhibitions about losing control. In such states, she became virtually possessed.

Another factor must be taken into account: that

with a female victim she also ceased to be a woman, and became a man. That is why it is possible to say that in the sexual orgies at 25 Cromwell Street it was Rose who took over the role that Paul Bernardo played in the kidnap of Leslie Mahaffy and Kristen French; it was she who became the eastern sultan, ordering her slaves to satisfy her whims, and exploding into brutality if they showed reluctance. The murders at 25 Cromwell Street were basically an expression of Rose West's power fantasy.

When Carol Ann Cooper's remains were uncovered in the cellar — the first of the victims to be buried there — the pathologist noted a deep gouge in the skull which suggested that she had been attacked with a knife. The skull wound may have been made by Fred West in dismembering the body. But if it was not made during the dismemberment, then it was probably made by Rose West while Carol was alive.

The next victim could hardly have been more different. Twenty-one-year old Lucy Partington, born on March 4, 1952, was a student of mediaeval English, who looked forward to an academic career. Her father, Roger Partington, was a lecturer in industrial chemistry, and her uncle was the novelist Kingsley Amis. But she was similar to all the other victims in that her mother and father had divorced; her mother lived with her second husband in a typical middle class home in the attractive village of Gretton, with its thatched roofs and Cotswold stone walls. And it was to Gretton that Lucy went to stay over the Christmas of 1973.

During her studies of the Middle Ages at Exeter University, Lucy had felt the attraction of Catholicism, and had become a Catholic convert. She was a serious-minded girl, who had never had a boyfriend. She tended to dress in polo-neck sweaters, corduroy trousers and hush puppies. Her friends were unable to persuade her to dress in anything more fashionable.

Gretton is about as far to the north-east of Cheltenham as Gloucester is to the south-west, and is — unfortunately for Lucy — only a few miles from Bishop's Cleeve. That Christmas of 1973, Lucy had attended midnight mass, and had been reading *Wuthering Heights*. But on the morning of December 27, she took a lift into the centre of Cheltenham with her brother David. She was on her way to see an old schoolfriend, Helen Render, who was badly disabled and unable to walk.

That evening, they talked about mediaeval art, and Lucy composed an application for a place at the Cortauld Institute in London. At about 10.15, Lucy said goodbye, and walked to a bus stop in the Evesham Road, about three minutes away. Helen told her that if she missed the bus, her father could give her a lift back home.

It is almost certain that Fred and Rose West were not out "hunting" that night. It is far more likely that they had paid a visit to Rose's parents at Bishop's Cleeve — in which case, the bus stop on the Evesham Road would be on their route home. They probably had eighteen-month-old Mae with them, and possibly Heather and Anne Marie. Lucy Partington would have felt perfectly safe accepting a lift from a young married couple with a car full of children.

But how would the Wests have overpowered her, with their children present? It is true that Lucy was a small girl, and would have been easy to subdue. But this was probably unnecessary. Lucy had accepted a lift from a car going in the wrong direction, so it seems likely that West claimed that he was returning to Bishop's Cleeve later, and offered her a lift back to

Gretton. Lucy would have accompanied them to Cromwell Street without suspicion, and probably accepted a cup of tea. The evidence for this is that when West confessed to killing her he seemed to know a great deal more about her than the other victims, suggesting that he had a chance to talk to her at length.

But perhaps the most ominous piece of evidence comes from the records of the Gloucestershire Royal Hospital. At 12.25 am on January 3, 1974, six days after Lucy Partington had been kidnapped, West walked into the hospital casualty department with a bad cut on his right hand. The likeliest explanation is that he sustained the cut while hacking up Lucy's body — in which case, it seems possible that Lucy was kept alive for almost a week. This well-educated girl with her upper-class accent may have intrigued and excited the Wests more than their previous victims, and the fact that she was almost certainly a virgin would have increased her attraction. They wanted time to savour her.

When her body was found in the cellar on March 6, 1994, there was a very sharp knife in the grave — probably the knife that injured West's hand. There was also the usual sticking plaster, indicating that her face had been bound with tape. She had been beheaded, and her right shoulder blade, a spinal bone, a left kneecap and three ribs were also missing.

Lucy's disappearance excited as much attention as that of Mary Bastholm and Carol Ann Cooper. Sniffer dogs and teams of police divers took part in the search; there were television appeals, and her mother Margaret commented: "How anyone could just vanish in three minutes completely baffles me." It would be twenty-one years before she would learn what had happened to her daughter. Lucy's friend

Helen Render would never find out — she died only two years later.

In their first year of kidnap-murder, the Wests had disposed of three victims; during the next six years there would be another five. They had acquired a taste for sex with unwilling partners.

Like Lucy Partington, Therese Siegenthaler was another "intellectual." Born in Trub, Switzerland, on November 27, 1952, she had been brought up speaking German. Like all the Wests' victims, she was the product of a broken home; her parents had divorced when Therese was 13. She held strong liberal opinions — particularly about Apartheid — and could be assertive. Like Lucy, Therese believed in plain dressing, and wore little or no make-up, and like Lucy, she wore horn-rimmed spectacles. Therese had studied judo, and felt she could handle predatory males. So when a friend advised her not to hitch-hike to Ireland in April, 1974, Therese told her that she could take care of herself.

Therese left her lodgings in Lewisham, south-east London, on April 16, 1974 — she was a sociology student at the Woolwich College of Further Education — and set out to hitch-hike to Holyhead, North Wales. From there she intended to take a boat to Ireland, where she would visit a priest with whom she shared strong views on South Africa, in Roscommon.

Like the others, Therese vanished without trace — until her skeleton was found in the Wests' cellar. She was the victim West called "Tulip", under the mistaken impression that she was Dutch. West had cut her into six pieces. As usual, fingers and toes were missing; so was a shoulder bone.

Her mother Klara did not live long enough to learn what had happened to Therese; she died after a heart attack in 1983; but she never had any doubt that her daughter was dead, saying on her death bed: "I am going to join Therese." Her ex-husband Fritz died from Alzheimer's disease in 1990.

It was Therese's younger sister Marianne who suspected the truth; she had often had appalling dreams of Therese screaming, and felt a conviction that her death "had something to do with sex." It was when a Swiss newspaper ran a story about the "House of Horror" that Marianne suddenly suspected that her sister had been a victim of Fred West, and when she saw a photograph of Lucy Partington she felt her blood run cold because it looked so much like Therese. Two weeks later, the police confirmed her fears when they rang her from Gloucester to tell her that her sister had been identified among the dead. Trying to deal with her grief, Marianne went to see a spiritualist, who told her that her sister's soul was at rest.

West would later "confess" to the police that Lucy Partington had been his mistress for some time, and that she was pregnant at the time of her murder — which, since Lucy was at Exeter University for the three months preceding her death, is obviously impossible.

Life at Cromwell Street seemed to proceed as usual. At the time of Therese's murder, Rose was four months pregnant, and in August she gave birth to Stephen. Pregnancy and giving birth had moderated her sexual demands. But by November these were as strong as ever. On November 14, the Wests went out hunting again.

At 15, Shirley Lloyd was their youngest murder victim. She had been born on June 26, 1959, but her parents separated two years later, and Shirley was taken into care; at the age of six, she was fostered by a Droitwich couple named Jim and Linda Hubbard.

She later adopted their name.

Again, like so many of the Wests' victims, Shirley was a rebel, and a month before her murder had run away from home, and been found camping in a field with a soldier. Then at a fairground she met an 18-year-old shopworker, Daniel Davies, and took him home to meet her foster parents.

Shirley was working on the makeup counter in Debenham's, in Worcester, six miles from her home in Droitwich, and on the evening of Friday, November 14, 1974, she met Daniel, and they bought fish and chips, and sat by the River Severn, kissing in the dark. At 8.30, Daniel saw her to her bus.

Since he watched the bus drive away, we can conclude that it was after Shirley had got off that she was forced into the Wests' car, and taken back to Cromwell Street. Tonight they felt like bizarre sex, and tape was wound in a mask around Shirley's face, and a plastic tube inserted in a nostril so she could breathe. When she was dead Fred carved off her head without bothering to remove the mask, or the tube from her nose, and threw it into the grave.

Her boyfriend Daniel was puzzled when Shirley failed to meet him the next day, but he assumed that she had decided not to see him any more, and made no attempt to contact her. By an odd coincidence, Daniel's elder brother Alan had once been the boyfriend of Carol Ann Cooper, whom he had met at a fair. Now Shirley joined Carol Ann Cooper, Lucy Partington and Therese Siegenthaler under the Wests' cellar floor. When her skeleton was found finger and toes were missing, and a part of her trunk.

In March 1975, Fred West again ran into trouble with the law; he was fined £50 for receiving stolen goods. In November he was again fined for receiving stolen goods, this time £75. In between these two appearances in court West murdered another teenage girl, who would become the fifth body in the basement.

Juanita Mott had been a lodger at 25 Cromwell Street. Like most other West victims, she was the product of a broken home, and like so many others, she was also a rebel — her sister commented: "She didn't like doing what anyone told her." She was born on March 1, 1957, the daughter of an American airman, Ernest Mott. By the time she was in her early teens, her parents had separated. She continued to live with her mother, Mary, but left home at 15 because they had strong disagreements.

She took a bedsit in Stroud Road, Gloucester, and there met Alan Davies, who was lodging at 25 Cromwell Street. The Wests had only just moved in. Three years later, in 1975, Juanita also moved into 25 Cromwell Street for a time. But she lost her factory job and, having no money, moved out to stay with a friend of the family called Jennifer Baldwin, who lived with her children in the nearby market town of Newent. On Saturday, April 12, 1975, Jennifer was due to get married, and Juanita agreed to babysit the children. But she decided to spend the previous evening in Gloucester, and hitch-hiked the eight and a half miles there in the late afternoon, telling her hostess: "I'll see you in the morning." It seems that she decided to visit her former lodging, and that the Wests were delighted by her unexpected arrival.

Once again there is evidence that Juanita was the victim of bizarre perversion. She was gagged with two nylon socks, a bra and two pairs of tights, then tied up with 17 feet of plastic-covered clothes-line, which was tied around her wrists and ankles, then around her skull in both directions, then round her body and thighs, so that she was bound hand and foot. A seven-foot length of rope with a noose was also found in the grave, and was probably used to suspend her from the beam.

Juanita Mott may have died of hanging. But there was also a skull fracture that seemed to have been inflicted by a ball pein hammer.

When she was dead West decapitated her and removed her legs. But again he kept back various parts of her body — some fingers and toes, as well as vertebrae and both kneecaps.

Finally, he dug yet another hole in the cellar floor, and threw in the rope and clothes-line as well as the body parts. His five victims had been buried clockwise, in date sequence. And since there was now no room for more corpses, he concreted the floor — with assistance from Rose's brother Graham — and turned it into a children's bedroom.

Oddly enough, Juanita's sister Belinda would later become a regular visitor at 25 Cromwell Street, without realising that her sister had been there before — and died there.

There is a three-year gap between the murder of Juanita Mott and that of the next known victim. This is unusual for serial killers, who usually go on until they are caught, and it is possible that, having filled up the cellar with bodies, Fred West began burying victims elsewhere. West was later to tell his son Stephen that there were other victims, but since he was virtually incapable of telling the truth, this cannot be taken as fact.

A short time after the murder of Juanita Mott, the Wests made the acquaintance of another potential victim, a 13-year old-girl we shall call Carol. But like Caroline Raine, Carol was to live to tell the tale; it was her evidence, along with that of that of Caroline and Anne Marie West, that played the central role in convicting Rose West.

Carol was — as usual — the child of a broken home; worse still, she had been sexually abused by her father and elder brother. And a man in his fifties had blackmailed her into having sex by threatening to tell the police that she had had under-age sex. Her various problems led to a care order, and in March 1975 she was placed in a home named Russet House, in Gloucester. During her time in Russet House she was taken to 25 Cromwell Street by an older girl from the same home. The Wests were by now allowing it to be known in the local children's homes that they were a hospitable couple who were always glad to offer a biscuit and an orange squash to bored or upset teenagers. On her first visit — where she met Rose and saw Fred in the distance — Rose seemed kindly and motherly (although, at 21, she was only eight years Carol's senior.)

After three months, Carol was moved to Jordan's Brook House, a children's home with an altogether tougher regime — presumably as some kind of punishment. Jordan's Brook was an approved school for delinquent girls. The residents were given points for good behaviour, and the number of points determined how much freedom they were allowed. Sounes reports that they often set off the fire alarm, since this caused the doors to unlock automatically, and they could run away. Most of its twenty-four residents hated and resented the regime.

Every three weeks, Carol was allowed home to see her mother in Tewkesbury; she began to make a habit of dropping in at 25 Cromwell Street on her way to the bus, and was always made welcome.

This continued for two years, and she had no reason to feel anything but gratitude to Rose West.

When she was 14, she had an affair with Rose's brother Graham, and later tried to convince him that she was pregnant by him. (Oddly enough, she claimed that she had no idea that Graham was Rose's brother — this seems to be yet another of those odd coincidences in the case.) The Wests sent her a birthday card on her fifteenth birthday. The only thing that bothered her slightly was Rose's tendency to turn the talk to sex — such questions as whether she combed her pubic hair and whether she masturbated.

In the summer of 1977, Carol ran away from Jordan's Brook House, and spent the night walking the streets of Gloucester. The following day, she called at Cromwell Street early in the evening, but there was no reply. She waited around in the park, and tried again at 11. This time the door was answered by Rose, wearing only a bra and panties. Carol explained that she had run away, and Rose invited her into the lounge. There, as Carol talked about her problems, Rose slipped an arm around her. "Then Rose started kissing me on my neck. I sort of pushed her away. She was touching my breasts outside my clothes. I struggled and she got up and went and got me a drink and a blanket. She was aware that her attention was unwelcome."

Carol fell asleep on the sofa, and the next morning had breakfast and left. Later that day she was picked up on the street by the police and returned to Jordan's Brook House. The escapade cost her her senior grading, and six weeks without being allowed out.

On her first weekend of freedom, she again called at 25 Cromwell Street on her way to the bus in the early afternoon. Rose, wearing a see-through blouse and miniskirt, invited her in. Some time later, Carol went upstairs to the toilet — she had a cyst on her bladder which made her incontinent; she left her wet knickers in the lavatory.

When she came out, Rose told her that there were two girls of her own age in another room. Carol described being taken into a bedroom with a cat o' nine tails on the wall, and pictures of humans having sex with animals. "As I walked in, I was stunned to see two girls naked in the room. One sat on the floor, the other was on the bed. Fred was in there as well, just wearing shorts." The younger girl — who looked about 14 — was blonde, with a 32 inch bust and painted toe nails. The elder looked about 16, and had black, short hair. Anne Marie would state in her book that she believes she was the dark-haired girl; although only 13 at the time, she looked older; but her memory had blotted out all recollection of the episode.

Rose put her arm around Carol, and said soothingly: "It's all right to feel and touch and to enjoy affection." Then she unzipped the girl's dress at the back, and went on to strip her naked, explaining that "they were all girls together."

After this, Rose began to do a strip-tease for Fred's benefit, removing her blouse and skirt seductively; Carol could see that Fred was aroused. She said she was terrified, yet also that she felt as if she had paid to go on a fairground ride, and could not get off until it stopped.

Fred produced packing tape, and bound the wrists of the blonde girl across her chest, after which she was turned on to her front. Then Fred pulled her legs apart so "it almost split her", and taped them down. Fred and Rose began to kiss; then Rose produced a vibrator, and penetrated the girl's anus so that she groaned in pain. Rose now removed Fred's underpants, and he spread the girl's buttocks and kissed her anus. As Carol looked away, she heard Fred give a groan of pleasure as he thrust into the girl — Carol was not sure whether he was having vaginal or anal intercourse. The girl was obviously in pain, and Carol said that her face wore a "help me" look. (The other girl — presumably Anne Marie — seemed to be "taking it in her stride".)

Fred now left the room to go to the toilet, and Rose untaped the girl on the bed, who began sucking her hair like a child, as if for comfort.

Now Rose approached Carol, and began running her hands over her body and pubic hair, kissing her neck and fondling her breasts. She was whispering words like "Enjoy." Carol remained frozen, and Rose commented: "I like stiff ones."

Carol was made to sit on the edge of the bed as Rose taped her wrists, then laid her down on her front. Meanwhile, Fred had returned, and was masturbating. As Carol buried her face in the brush-nylon sheets, she felt her ankles being taped apart. Then Rose ran the vibrator down Carol's back, and around her vagina, asking: "Is that nice, Fred?"

Carol felt female fingers with long nails enter her vagina, while the other hand caressed her breasts and twisted a nipple. Rose was continuing to murmur: "Enjoy." Rose felt inside her for a long time, as if conducting a medical examination. Then Carol felt something cold enter her anus — she thought it was the neck of a bottle, or a candle she had seen earlier — and experienced great pain. "I felt my anus was being split. I heard a popping sound."

After the object was removed, Fred climbed on to her and entered her vagina; at the same time, Rose caressed Fred's penis. As he began to gasp that he was coming, Rose told him to pull it out and climax on her back. Fred withdrew, and Carol felt the sticky droplets in the small of her back. Rose rubbed them in. Then Rose snipped the tape with tiny scissors, cutting Carol's thumb, and Carol was allowed to get up.

She took her dress to the bathroom and pulled it on; in the mirror she could see that she had a trickle of blood coming from her anus. Carol hurried out of the house without bothering to take her shoes, and caught the bus.

Back at home in Tewskebury, her mother berated her for being late, and Carol was aggressive and angry — more so because she felt too ashamed to tell of what had happened. She went to her bedroom and rocked back and forth, her knees under her chin.

Six weeks later, still simmering with rage, she took a can with some petrol back to Cromwell Street, intending to burn down the house; but at the last moment her courage failed her.

After her rape by the Wests, Carol's life failed to improve. She would marry twice, but both husbands were violent, and she had to seek refuge in a home for battered wives. Six years after her rape at 25 Cromwell Street, she attempted suicide, and was given electro-convulsive therapy. She was also treated for gonorrhea. In 1993 she was found wandering around Basingstoke, and in 1994 ended up in Southampton, where she was assaulted again. She was to tell the police after her afternoon at the Wests: "I couldn't trust anybody after this."

Anne Marie was another long-term victim of Fred and Rose. She began to menstruate when she was nine, and was not allowed to wear sanitary towels. When she was about ten, she learned that her stepmother was a prostitute when her father beckoned to her one day and said: "I've got something I want to show you." He took her to the door of Rose's bedroom, and quietly removed a plaque with a small screwdriver. Then Anne Marie was told to look through a spy hole in the door. Rose was on the bed with a black man. Anne Marie was shocked — and even more shocked as her father peered through the hole, obviously in a state of intense excitement.

Not long after this, Anne Marie was made to prostitute herself to Rose's clients, mostly West Indians. (To call them clients is not entirely accurate, for Rose never took money at this time; the sex sessions were purely for her own — and Fred's — enjoyment.) Rose stayed in the room while this was going on, afraid that Anne Marie would reveal her age. There were about five "regulars", one a black man in his sixties who, after Fred's arrest, was charged with having sex with Anne Marie on many occasons when she was ten. (The charge was later dropped.)

Another of Rose's lovers so liked Anne Marie that he brought her a box of chocolates. Rose confiscated them, and ate every one of them in front of her. Anne Marie's admirer never returned — Rose was determined that only she should be the centre of attraction at 25 Cromwell Street.

A curious episode occurred when Anne Marie was thirteen. Rose invited her out to an evening at a pub — possibly with the idea of picking up men. They were driven by Fred to a pub on the outskirts of Gloucester, and left there. Rose then plied Anne Marie with Gold Label barley wine; when Anne Marie pulled a face, Rose snapped: "Don't moan — just fucking drink it." But as the evening proceeded, Anne Marie could hardly believe her friendliness. "We were both laughing and joking." Rose was flirting with a group of men, but it was suddenly clear that they were uncomfortable — perhaps Rose had intimated her intentions too clearly.

At 10.30 they left the pub, and Fred picked them up in his van. As soon as Rose and Anne Marie were in the back, Rose began tearing her clothes off and hitting her — evidently something Anne Marie had done had enraged her. Fred stopped the van, climbed in the back, and joined in the beating. Rose was shouting that Anne Marie was mistaken if she thought they could laugh and joke together. Then she held Anne Marie down while Fred raped her.

Only Rose West can now explain what she and Fred had in mind that night. Did she want to introduce herself and Anne Marie to the men in the pub as a mother-and-daughter prostitution team? And did Anne Marie perhaps spoil it by blurting out her real age in her drunken euphoria?

But usually Fred was careful that Rose should not find out that he was having sex with Anne Marie. He took her as an assistant on building jobs, and had sex with her when they were alone in a house, and also in the back of the van. She emphasised that the sex was "normal", and that her father kissed her on the mouth. "It was almost as if I was his girlfriend, not his daughter." For some reason, West always switched on a purple light on the dashboard when he wanted sex, and Anne Marie said that it always gave her a "funny feeling in her stomach." After sex, he would apologise, give her pocket money, and tell her not to tell Rose. On all these occasions, West never used a contraceptive.

Rose undoubtedly knew Fred well enough to suspect what was happening, which may be why, in June 1979, she made an attempt to provide Anne Marie with a regular boyfriend. She had taken Anne Marie out to a pub called The Famous Pint Pot; at this time Rose would have been 25, and Anne Marie was a month short of her fifteenth birthday, although she looked older. When Rose saw two young men sitting together, she lost no time in asking if they could join them. One of them was a powerfully-built factory worker called Mike Spencer, who was 21. "From then on", Mike told the *Daily Mirror*, "things moved very quickly. We chatted and were getting on quite well. Rosemary was quite well-dressed, making lots of sexy comments."

Before closing time, Anne Marie went to the Ladies, and Rose turned to Mike Spencer and asked: "Would you like to come and stay the night at our place? You can sleep with my daughter." When Anne Marie came back Rose nodded to her, and then Mike Spencer left the pub with them.

Back in Cromwell Street, without further delay, Anne Marie and Mike Spencer went to the basement bedroom, got undressed, and climbed into bed. He comments that "she looked about 18, and seemed quite experienced."

Mike was worried about how her father might react the next morning, and was relieved when Fred West seemed casual and friendly. In fact, West liked making new acquaintances; he could usually persuade them to provide him with something he needed at half price, or — as in the case of Mike Spencer — get them to help him in his building work. Mike helped Fred West to build a wall in his back garden, and posed for a photograph with his mistress's father.

Mike Spencer continued to sleep with Anne Marie during the next three months, becoming a regular visitor at 25 Cromwell Street. He describes how during one Sunday lunch Fred West started talking about pimping and prostitution "and all types of sex." "He talked about women, and what he liked doing to them in bed."

Mike also noted that Anne Marie liked to wear a red outfit that struck him as rather "tarty." He added: "But I didn't care, because I was getting what I wanted — sex."

The affair came to an end one day after a visit to a fairground. A man came over to Anne Marie and whispered to her. Anne Marie said indignantly: "I don't do that kind of thing any more" — verifying Mike's suspicion that she had been a prostitute. "It was then I thought I should get out of the relationship and left her a day later."

During the following year, Anne Marie began to bleed from the vagina and to feel ill. Finally, she told Rose, who took her to see a doctor; then she was taken to Gloucester Hospital. It seemed to her that the nurses were distant and unfriendly. She was told that she was going to be put to sleep so they could look inside her. When she woke up on the ward she was feeling dizzy and sick, with a drip attached to her arm. She spent another week there without visitors. It was only in later years that she saw her medical records and realised that she had suffered an ectopic pregnancy (a pregnancy in a fallopian tube) and had been aborted. The nurses had been unfriendly because they felt she was a teenage tart who had got what she deserved.

Anne Marie decided to run away from home soon after she came out of hospital. Her decision was precipitated by another clash with Rose. Anne Marie's stomach was still stitched up when Rose decided that she could start doing housework again. As Anne Marie was hoovering, Rose became increasingly irritable. When Anne Marie apologised, Rose said: "Don't be fucking sorry. Do it fucking right." Suddenly she exploded, flinging Anne Marie to the floor, then kicking her in the stomach, shouting: "Stupid cow." "Her face was a picture of evil, her eyes filled with rage but with that strange dead look behind them."

Soon after that, at three o'clock in the morning, Anne Marie crept down the stairs and walked into the night. She found an all-night cafe, and had tea and toast, then spent the rest of the night in the park. After a few days without a roof over her head, she stayed with a schoolfriend who had a room; but the landlord threw her out. She admits that she was desperate for a home, and that "to get it I used the only method I had — sex." Life was extremely hard. But at least she was free. She states in *Out of the Shadows* her conviction that if she had not walked out of the house she would have left it eventually — like her sister Heather — in a wooden box.

8

THE CHILDREN

One evening in the late spring of 1977, Rose West picked up a teenage prostitute named Shirley Robinson in a Gloucester pub, and brought her back to Cromwell Street for lesbian sex — Shirley made no secret about being bisexual.

Shirley Ann Robinson was small — just over five feet tall — and plump, with a round face, but she was not unpretty. She had been born in Rutland on October 8, 1959, the daughter of an RAF corporal, Roy Robinson. Shirley was only three when her mother walked out, taking her daughter with her, but the child was soon back with her father. Like so many of the Wests' victims, she had been difficult and rebellious, and when she was fifteen went back to live with her mother in Hartlepool. But her mother was unable to cope with her, and she was taken into care by the Bristol Social Services. She became a juvenile delinquent, shoplifting for cigarettes and food, and drifted inevitably into prostitution. At 18, Shirley felt that life had treated her badly, and was described by a social worker as "exremely withdrawn and sullen." She had affairs with a number of lesbians, usually many years her senior.

Fred and Rose offered her a room on the first floor of the house, overlooking the back garden where she would eventually be buried. They both found the idea of having a live-in lover exciting, and Shirley, delighted to have some kind of security, made sure that she pleased them both.

In October 1977 Shirley realised she was pregnant. Fred was delighted. Rose was also pregnant at the time — although the baby would prove to be coloured — and he felt proud of his "two women", telling one visitor: "This is my wife, and this" (indicating Shirley) "is my lover."

Shirley became increasingly attached to Fred, sending her father in Germany a photograph of the two of them and telling him: "This is the man I am going to marry ... I have never been so happy in my life." And Fred occasionally teased Rose, telling her that Shirley was going to be his next wife.

But Fred and Rose were too close for anyone else to come between them. And when Shirley began to press Fred to divorce Rose he became increasingly hostile. He told Rose's brother-in-law Jim Tyler: "Shirley is mooning about and hanging around me all the time. Rose just won't stand for it. She's got to fucking go."

Shirley was becoming aware of the increasing atmosphere of hostility, and began to spend her nights on the settee of another lodger, Liz Brewer, afraid that Rose would attack her in the night. Liz was heterosexual, and made it clear to Shirley that she had no interest in lesbian sex; the two nevertheless became good friends.

For Shirley it was a depressing situation, another typical blow from fate. Her lover was obviously tired of her and her lover's wife — who had now given birth — detested her. It was no time to be eight months pregnant.

On April 10, 1978, Shirley claimed Sickness

Benefit for her pregnancy, and on May 2 saw her GP, Dr John Buckley, who told her about various other benefits she might be eligible for. The baby was due in June. On May 9 Shirley and Liz Brewer went to a photograph booth in Woolworths to get their pictures taken; Liz stuck out her tongue and Shirley widened her eyes until they bulged.

On May 10 Shirley again spent the night on Liz Brewer's settee. They had arranged to meet friends, but Shirley decided that she would prefer a lie-in, and Liz went alone to see the friends. When she returned at tea-time she was staggered when Fred told her that Shirley had left during the day, and gone to live with her father in Germany. At that moment Shirley's body was undoubtedly hidden in a corner of the cellar. The next day Rose was seen emptying out the possessions from Shirley's room into bin bags. Later, Shirley's room was turned into Rose's "lounge", with a bar in one corner with a black magic sign on top, tiger skins on the floor and a chandelier light.

Since there was no more space in the cellar, West was forced to bury Shirley Robinson in the garden. The skeleton of the foetus lay separated from her bones — West would tell the unlikely story that he had cut it from her womb in an attempt to save its life. Oddly enough, no hair was found in the grave, suggesting that he might have scalped her. Fred West undoubtedly derived some strange pleasure from treating corpses as playthings.

Soon after her murder the local social services received a claim in Shirley's name for maternity benefit. Since Shirley had already claimed, the office made enquiries at 25 Cromwell Street, and the visitor was told that she no longer lived there. Rose — probably urged on by Fred — had decided to try and claim for Shirley's dead baby.

In retrospect, it is not difficult to understand how Shirley came to be a murder victim. West's attitude towards the opposite sex was that of the high-dominance predator; when he looked at any woman, he fantasised about what it would be like to undress her. But once his curiosity is satisfied, the high-dominance predator tends to lose interest — unless, as Maslow discovered, the female is in his own dominance group. No account of Shirley Robinson suggests that she belonged to the dominant 5%. She seems to have been — like Ann McFall and Rena West — a typical medium-dominance female, dreaming of "Mr Right" and longing for security. So when the initial pleasure of having a live-in mistress had worn off, West would have quickly tired of her. To have her "mooning" about him and dropping hints about marriage would have been the last straw. And the notion of exchanging Rose for Shirley would have been unthinkable — he liked Rose's hardness and lack of sentimentality.

If Shirley had had the sense to recognise her danger, and allow the Wests to feel that she represented no threat, she might have lived on in safety at Cromwell Street, and given birth to her baby. As it was, they were both tired of her, and saw no obvious way of ridding themselves of the nuisance. As Fred said: "She's got to go."

For the children, life at Cromwell Street went on as usual. It is a relief to turn from the evidence of rapes, floggings and murders to the account given by Mae and Stephen in *Inside 25 Cromwell Street*. The main thing that emerges from this book — put together from interviews — is that Fred was such a habitual liar that even his children knew that their father could never be relied on to tell the truth, and a thief who would steal anything that was not nailed down. Mae declares: "He would see a pile of bricks or cement in the road and go back that night when it was dark and load them into his van. Practically the whole of our house extension was made from stolen goods, right down to the wooden support beams that held the roof up. He was quite open about it; he never liked to pay for anything.

"When he did repair jobs in people's houses, he'd leave a latch open on a window and later that night he'd steal objects he'd liked the look of. Our house was full of ornaments that he'd claim he'd been given by a satisfied customer. At one time he had seven video recorders, the same number of televisions, and loads of radio cassette players in the house ... At least 99% of the contents of the house were stolen, including the lino on the floor."

Stephen tells how his father stole building material from his boss Derek. "If Dad got his hands on some blue paint, the whole house would be done up with it. It was the same with a cheap bit of carpet. The whole hallway would be done up with Derek's stuff, and when he came round, we had to put up sheets to hide everything that Dad had pinched ... It was a compulsion, just like a magpie which steals anything that's shiny and available. He didn't need the stuff he stole, most of it was useless."

"We had to go out with Dad on a Sunday", Mae recalls, "and run across a field to steal a bale of hay. The three of us kids ran like crazy and threw it into the back of Dad's van. He would syphon off some poor bloke's petrol on the way back home ... "

Stephen tells how they were taken to a park in Cheltenham to steal bicycles. "He would walk 100 yards in front of me and break the bike lock very quickly ... I'd have to follow behind and ride the bike to the van ... We'd get them for the whole family. To be honest, I never thought we were doing anything wrong. It was normal family life for us."

West had a curious streak of meanness, a determination not to spend a penny if it could be avoided. For Christmas the children got only one present. They never received spending money. For entertainment they went to the fountains in the centre of Gloucester and groped around for the two-pence pieces that people had thrown in for good luck.

Holidays were cheap, for they always went camping at the same place, Barry Island in south Wales, for seven consecutive years. "It was really to give Mum a break ... she didn't sleep with other men on holiday." They would travel in a van, sitting in the back on carpet or the wheel arches. It was necessary to stop every two hours so the children could stretch their legs. Mae says: "It was always raining in Barry Island. You knew you were approaching Wales because you could see the rain clouds."

They were never given spending money — their holiday consisted in sitting on the beach or dipping briefly in the freezing sea. For lunch they had sandwiches — one each — and a flask of tea. The elder children would go for long walks.

One evening Stephen and Mae returned with some friends they had made, but as they approached the four-berth caravan they saw it was rocking and shaking, and heard loud screams. As they came closer they saw that a curious crowd had gathered around. It was Fred and Rose having sex in their usual uninhibited way.

Anne Marie decribes, how, in the summer of 1976, Rose went with her father Bill and several of the children to a holiday campsite at Westward Ho! in North Devon. Anne Marie had won the Miss Princess of Devon competition, and was looking forward to the parade at the end of the week. But Rose, in her best nymphomaniac form, had "worked her way through the orchestra like a dose of salts. She was having it away night after night, either in her chalet or in theirs, and it was becoming the joke of the camp." Rose's father, as possessive as ever, exploded into fury, and the next day they packed their bags and left.

The holidays seem to have been the one time when West dropped his objection to the children playing together. At home, his obsession with total control meant that he preferred to keep them apart. "He'd say there was something wrong with us if we were laughing and playing together. He didn't like us talking to Mum, especially me. I wasn't allowed to talk to her alone for some reason," said Stephen.

On one occasion, Stephen, Mae and Heather were ordered to stop talking after they had been put to bed in the cellar. When their parents overheard them talking again, they took the three children — aged 5, 6 and 7 — and thrust them out of the front door. It was cold and rainy, and they were left there for more than fifteen minutes before they were allowed back in.

Some of their stories are funny. West was putting up curtains, standing on a chair that had been a present from Rose's mother. He leaned too far forward, and the chair fell over, the back hitting him in the stomach. He fell to the ground, unable to get his breath. When Rose, summoned by the children, came running in, he gasped: "Your mum's trying to kill me. She always hated me."

Mae's account of her father's eating habits is worth quoting. "He'd cut a huge end off a loaf and put big slabs of cheese on top. He'd eat an onion like it was an apple. He'd also spread a thick lump of lard from the chip pan on to a piece of bread, and eat the thick, really blubbery part of the meat. It was awful what he'd eat. Mum is really fussy about what she cooks, and if she didn't like the look of something, she'd just chuck it in the bin. Dad would shout, "No, Rose, that's perfect", then he'd grab the bin and start eating out of it, and he'd offer it to us kids."

This undoubtedly reflects his starving childhood; but an obsession with food is also characteristic of certain "sex maniacs" — for example, when Sade was confined in an asylum, he became monstrously gross; he was "sublimating" his craving for sex in food. (Attendants in the asylum complained that Sade's conversation consisted of endlessly obscene variations on sex — another point of resemblance to West.)

It was Mae who claimed that her mother had switched to full-time paid prostitution in the mid-1980s, advertising herself in sex magazines as "Mandy", with a notice: "Sexy housewife needs it deep and hard from VWE (very well endowed) male, while husband watches — coloureds welcome." "Mum started to get her flat together upstairs and she spent a lot of money on it. There was this one man in particular who used to come to our house all the time, he was one of the freebies. He was one of Dad's old friends, and used to come around whenever it suited him, usually Sunday lunch time. Mum didn't even like him — she said it made her sick going to bed with him — but Dad made her do it. He used to grind her down, night after night, telling her she was a bad wife if she didn't do things for her husband."

Other regular lovers included a man with a glass eye and one with a wooden leg.

"Every Sunday Mum cooked dinner and he always

came round when she was preparing it. We knew when the doorbell went on a Sunday what was going to happen next. It really used to piss us off because it would be a really nice dinner, and when Mum went upstairs, Dad would finish cooking it, and he always ruined it. There would be lumps in the gravy that were like potatoes underneath, but they were corn-flour balls when you cut them up. Once I was old enough I'd take over the cooking instead, but I had to physically fight him off to do it."

While Rose was upstairs with her black lover, Fred would sit on the settee, listening to what was going on in the bedroom through a speaker pressed against his ear. "We used to keep turning up the television to drown out the groaning noises from upstairs."

If Fred came home from work while Rose was upstairs, he immediately unwound the loudspeaker wire so he could listen in, or went to listen at the door.

Stephen comments that "she made a note of what she charged, and it seemed as if she gave them marks out of ten. It was written very neatly in rows, like accounts. She also used to order men from the book. If she fancied a coloured bloke who was well endowed she would look it up and ring him instead. You could hear her call, and count the minutes until there was a ring at the door.

"There was a red album, and also a money box with a key ... When I opened it, I found a bundle of pictures of Dad lying naked on the bed, and Mum naked with other men."

After Rose's arrest, a Jamaican named Andrew Angus told the *Sunday Mirror* how he had become Rose's lover. He was walking past 25 Cromwell Street in the afternoon when Rose came out and asked him if he knew anything about televisions. He went into the house to see what was wrong. "When I turned round. Rosemary was standing there in the living room, naked apart from some revealing underwear."

Clearly, for purposes of seduction, Rose departed from her normal practice of not wearing knickers.

"I remember she put the video on, which had some hardcore sex scenes in it, and she started to kiss me. Before I knew it, we were upstairs on her double bed. I put a condom on, and we began having sex. There was a huge mirror covering nearly all the ceiling, and the bed itself was massive ... I hardly knew her, and there we were in her bed having sex."

Like all Rose's self-chosen lovers, Andrew Angus was not charged for sex.

Rose seemed obsessed by Jamaicans and Jamaican music. "She was turned on by black men. She showed me a picture of one of her children — a half-caste young girl — and seemed proud that she was half black.

"Her husband Fred knew I slept with his wife, but he didn't seem bothered at all. Rosemary said she had a very open relationship, and said her husband did not mind her sleeping with other men."

The only exception was when Rose decided she wanted to open up the relationship further, and took a room nearby; as soon as Fred found out, he put a stop to it. It was important to him to have absolute control.

Andrew Angus described how he often had three-hour sex sessions with Rose West. "Rosemary was totally sex mad. She always knew exactly what she wanted and how to get it. She loved sex. When I slept with her, she was very demanding. I was always exhausted afterwards."

Nothing could be clearer than this. Unlike the

majority of members of her profession, Rose was a prostitute because she was sex mad. A decade and a half of living with a man who thought about sex from the moment he woke up to the moment he went to bed had turned a dominant but normally-sexed woman into a nyphomaniac. What he now wanted was for his children to join in. Mae tells how:

" ... once when I opened my bedroom door as one client was passing, Mum pushed me back in, but not before he had the chance to ask if 'that one was available.' I was only about thirteen. Mum kicked this guy straight out. But when Dad found out he was really keen and said 'that's a good idea.' "

The Wests filmed their orgies, and Fred liked to watch the videos afterwards. Stephen tells how he found a video of Rose sitting on the kitchen table with her legs wide apart, using a vibrator on herself, then urinating all over tea towels on the table. "They also took videos of Mum with other men in the back of the van when she was tied up. Dad tied mum up, whipped her, and then had sex with her."

So mutual flogging — Rose also tied up Fred and whipped him — was a basic part of the Wests' sexual repertoire. This helps us to understand what went on when they had abducted a victim. The girl was tied up — because the sight of bondage sexually excited them both — and tape was bound round her face because it was yet another form of bondage. Then the victim was suspended from the beam in the cellar by her wrists, so that she looked like some slave about to be flogged by a perverted Roman emperor. In effect, the Wests were orchestrating their own fantasy. And if the girls had been willing victims, who participated of their own free will, they would not have been killed.

This becomes clear from the testimony of another

witness, Mary Kathryn Halliday, who became involved with the Wests in October 1988. She told her story to the *Sunday Mirror* on March 13, 1994, which begins:

"There was only one rule when Mary Halliday joined Fred and Rose West for a wild three-in-a-bed sex session — never on a Thursday. That was the day when part-time prostitute Rose turned her home into a vice den, entertaining up to six men a day.

"Mary, 37, revealed last night how she was seduced at the House of Horror, and took part in the passionate romps until the couple's jealousy over her ended the twice daily sessions. She said: "Their kinky games went too far and I didn't want to play any more."

Mary Halliday was living in lodgings at 11 Cromwell Street; her marriage had just broken up, and she was "deeply unhappy about her sexuality and very vulnerable." She needed someone to repair a leak in her bathroom, and sent for Fred West.

"He turned up in paint-spattered overalls and sandals ... He was full of chat, a real Jack-the-Lad. By the time he finished, he had asked me to go round and meet "the missus.""

Fred had apparently been told that Mary Halliday was bisexual, and explained that Rose also "liked a bit of both."

Fred took Mary home with him, and offered her drinks downstairs. Then he asked her if she would like to see the bar. He took her to a room off the main hallway. It was then that Rose joined them.

"As soon as she walked in I wondered what I had got myself into. She was plump, busty, not very attractive, and wearing dark-rimmed glasses and a tiny miniskirt. When she sat down next to me she wiggled down, so that her skirt slid up around the top of her thighs. She wasn't wearing anything underneath. She kept nestling up against me and getting closer. She couldn't walk past me without brushing up against me.

"About half an hour later, after Fred had poured me several large drinks, she took me by the hand and led me upstairs. Fred walked right behind me so I couldn't go back.

"Rose was very aggressive, by far the dominant one. We all took our clothes off, and had sex until three in the morning." This sex included Rose and Mary Halliday using vibrators and dildos on one another.

By that time, the cellar had been turned into the children's bedroom — the seven children, aged 7 to 11, slept in bed partitioned off by wooden panelling. Mary was taken to see it on her second visit, after which they all went upstairs and had sex again.

"Rose was absolutely insatiable. She used to say that no woman or man could ever satisfy her. I don't think she got much sexual pleasure from Fred — he wasn't very well endowed.

"That time, Fred just wanted to watch. He walked around the bed, and on occasions would climb on to it, but just to get a closer look. Rose only had to look at my empty glass and he would go down and refill it."

In the course of that night, Fred asked her if she would like to see their "secret room." She was taken across the hallway and into a room with a huge four-poster bed. Rose took a suitcase of magazines out of a wardrobe. It was full of pictures of black latex suits, with holes for the nose and mouth. Also in the suitcase were suits exactly like the pictures. Their worn appearance made it clear that they had been used.

"Rose and Fred described all the items in detail — they were very turned on by talking about them. We were all naked, and I felt embarrassed." The Wests wanted to know if Mary would be willing to wear one of the suits, and "dish out punishment."

"The bedroom cupboard was filled with sex toys, and I realised I was totally out of my depth."

In the mornings, Rose would take the children to nursery school, then knock on the window of Mary Halliday's ground-floor flat at about 9.30. Mary would then go to her house, and they would have coffee, and then go upstairs and make love until midday. On one occasion, as they came downstairs, they met Mae, who introduced herself as Rose's daughter, and did not seem in the least surprised to see her mother coming from the bedroom with a woman.

"Fred used to come home in the evenings and join in. But I only had sex with him three or four times, because he preferred to watch.

"I never saw him and Rose make love, even when we were three in a bed. Their relationship was very strange. On the surface they seemed a normal respectable couple. They were popular in the street, and people used to talk to them, or Fred would go to their houses to do odd jobs."

Soon Fred was pressing Mary to move in. He wanted another *ménage à trois*, like the one with Shirley Robinson that had ended more than ten years earlier. Fred was now approaching fifty; Rose was 36; but their sexual appetites were as feverish as ever. But then Fred told her that no pets were allowed, and she decided against it.

The *Sunday Mirror* account declares that the Wests and Mary Halliday drifted apart because they began quarrelling about Mary's affections — a story that sounds psychologically improbable, since neither of them were the type to become emotionally attached to a third party. An account in the *Daily Mirror* of January 3, 1995, tells a more plausible story.

"He became more and more violent and demanding. He enjoyed tying me up and putting a pillow over my face. He whipped me and tried to abuse me with huge sex objects." And on one occasion West put a pillow over her face and cut her stomach with a knife.

She was also worried about their "torture chamber", a room with whips, chains and hooks. He also showed her home videos of young girls being whipped, tortured and humiliated. "One of them was young and blonde. She was in pain, and obviously terrified." This sounds like the young blonde that "Carol" saw being raped twelve years earlier. Yet Mary Halliday mentions that there were two or three videos of her, which suggests that she came back on more than one occasion, and acted the part of the terrified victim. The fact that West showed these videos to Mary Halliday certainly suggests that the blonde was not a murder victim.

But Rose also joined in the games of sadism. Mary Halliday tells how Rose placed a pillow over her head, and whispered: "What does it feel like not being able to see?" And she adds the significant sentence: "They got their thing from seeing other people frightened." She confirms that Rose joined in with Fred's strange assaults with sexual objects and whips — all confirming that, as a result of endless games of bondage, flogging and whipping, Rose had become as much addicted to sadism as her husband.

All this amounts to what the sexual psychologist Magnus Hirschfeld labels "minor sadism", which is essentially a game of "let's pretend" — unlike the "true sadism" of killers like Peter Kürten and Pee

Wee Gaskins, which involved smashing victims' skulls with hammers, strangling children, and burning holes in them with boiling lead.

On the other hand, the fact that West's sexual demands became more and more violent, and included cutting Mary's stomach with a knife, suggests that minor sadism could sometimes turn into true sadism. Excited by flogging and whipping, West may well have gone further than he intended, and ended by killing the girls, or injuring them so seriously that they had to be killed.

Mary — who, the article explains, now lives with a female partner in Berkshire — "stopped going around to see them, and in the end we didn't speak. We ignored one another if we met in the street." The relationship ended in June 1989, after nine months.

When Fred West was first arrested, Mary Halliday did not connect these reports of a mass murderer with the man with whom she had sex five years earlier. It was only when the metal sign that read "25 Cromwell Street" appeared on the television screen with a picture of Fred that she realised, and spilt her coffee in her lap.

Even before Shirley Robinson's murder in May 1978, Fred decided to make Rose pregnant again; the result was a baby girl, Louise, born on November 17, 1978.

Meanwhile, Fred had been forgiven by Rose's father Bill Letts for stealing his daughter, and the two had gone into business. When Letts decided to take early retirement from Smith's Industries in Bishop's Cleeve, he was given a considerable redundancy payment. His first reaction was to use up some of it enjoying himself; Sounes says that he travelled around Devon "living the high life", but that after two years he became ill and returned home.

Recognising that, whatever Fred's faults, he was an obsessively hard worker, he proposed that they should go into partnership. Their first venture, a cleaning business, failed, and they decided to try again with a cafe, which Fred would renovate. In due course, this also failed. It was in this cafe that Fred told Rose's brother-in-law Jim Tyler that Shirley Robinson would "have to go."

A year later, in the spring of 1979, Bill Letts became ill with a lung complaint contracted in the Plymouth naval yard; he died on May 24, 1979. Not long before this, his son Graham had walked in to find that his father had pinned his mother Daisy against the wall and was slapping her face. He remained a violent man to the end. At his funeral, Rose scandalised everyone by turning up in a miniskirt and stiletto heels; but her brother recalls that she seemed genuinely moved — the only one member of the family who felt any regret at seeing the last of a tyrant who had made their lives a misery. Daisy Letts was to say that he had made his own life miserable, and that she always felt he was a weak character. Bill Letts's last words to his son Graham were: "Don't get married to the wrong person."

In prison, Fred West was to accuse Bill Letts of playing some part in the murders. That certainly sounds like another of West's inventions. But there can be no doubt that Bill Letts became very closely involved in the sex lives of his daughter and son-in-law. Wansell states: "Letts, almost certainly, became one of the men whom West would invite to participate in the sadistic sexual practices that he carried out in the cellar of Cromwell Street." And he quotes West as saying that Letts never "abused" his daughter — "she was more willing than he was. I caught them at least half a dozen times, and she was enjoying it." On a holiday in Devon, all three slept in the same bed, and Fred was able to satisfy his voyeurism watching Bill Letts make love to his own daughter. So the question of whether Bill Letts played an active role in the torture and murder at 25 Cromwell Street must be left open.

Sixteen-year-old Alison Chambers was the last of the Wests' murder victims during the 1970s.

Like so many other victims, Alison was the child of a broken home, and a rebel who resented attempts to make her conform to authority. She had been born in Hildesheim, Germany, on September 8, 1962, the daughter of Robert Chambers, a sergeant in the Royal Army Ordnance Corps, and of a private in the Women's Royal Army Corps. By the time Alison was eight, the marriage was over, and her parents were engaged in a bitter divorce. Her mother Joan went home to Swansea, while her husband stayed on in Germany with their three daughters. A custody battle ended with the three girls being returned to their mother in Swansea.

Alison found it hard to settle. She had been a good student, excellent in art and literature — she also wrote poetry — but now she became difficult to handle, staying out late — sometimes all night — with her boyfriend. Her stepfather often had to go out searching for her after returning home from a twelve-hour shift at work. Eventually, in exasperation, her mother — who was pregnant again — decided that the fourteen-year-old should be taken into care. Alison seems to have taken this decision cheerfully, perhaps hoping that she would have more freedom away from home. When she was disillusioned she began absconding from the home — on one occasion she got as far as Paddington Station. The result was that at the age of 16 she was transferred to the

Jordan's Brook House in Gloucester — the children's home that "Carol" had found so oppressive.

Alison hated it, and continued to abscond — seven times in eight months. Her dream was to live on a farm, where she could lie in the deep grass and write poetry. She spent much of her time leading a fantasy life, and the others made fun of her.

A girl named Anne took her to 25 Cromwell Street to visit a friend there. Alison was a pretty girl, with shoulder-length hair, and Rose West found her attractive. And Alison, like "Carol", was delighted to have a "big sister" who offered her a shoulder to cry on. When Rose found out about her dreams of living on a farm, she told her that she and Fred owned a farm, and showed her a picture from an estate agent's brochure. When Alison was 17, she said, she could come and work on the farm and ride horses and write poetry. Alison was completely taken in — after all, why should this sympathetic mother of five children lie to her?

She told other girls at the children's home that she had met an older man who was in love with her; they assumed it was the kind of fantasy that Alison was prone to. On August 5, 1979, Alison absconded for the eighth time. The next day she failed to appear at the lawyer's office where was was employed on a youth training scheme. But she was not killed immediately, for she wrote to her mother in Swansea saying that she had met a "nice homely family" who wanted her to come and work as a nanny. She said that they had a daughter almost her own age — this would be Anne Marie, then fourteen — who regarded her as a big sister. In a few weeks time she would be 17, and able to go and live on the Wests' farm ...

This letter was forwarded to the Glamorgan Social

Services, who decided that since Alison would soon be 17, no further action would be taken.

But the Wests had no intention of allowing her to live that long — otherwise they would not have told her the fairy tale about their farm. One night Alison Chambers was subjected to the same kind of ordeal as the earlier victims, gagged with a three-inch-wide purple fashion belt that passed under her chin and over the top of her head, tied up, and raped, flogged and finally murdered.

Alison's body was the second to be found, soon after that of Heather West; Fred himself pointed out the place, outside the ground-floor bathroom. The grave was full of mud, and the bones were jumbled up. But once again her killer had kept back a number of her bones, including both kneecaps, two of her ribs, her ankles and toes, and part of her thoracic vertebrae.

Alison Chambers was the last of Fred West's known sex-murder victims. The only other death for which he is known to be responsible was that of his daughter Heather, eight years later.

It is unusual for serial sex killers to stop voluntarily — in fact, virtually unknown. In most such cases the murders — which to begin with take place at fairly long intervals — are spaced closer and closer together, as if the killer is possessed by a kind of frenzy. The Seattle serial killer Ted Bundy escaped from prison near Chicago after twenty or more murders, and found his way to Florida, where he assumed a new identity; yet he was unable to stop killing, and went on another "murder spree" that soon ended in his arrest. Richard Ramirez, the "Night Stalker" of Los Angeles, killed once in 1984, and began killing again in the spring of 1985, claiming seven victims in the month before his capture. The Milwaukee necrophile Jeffrey Dahmer killed a dozen young men in his last eighteen months of freedom, the last two in a period of five days.

One of the very few known cases of a serial killer ceasing to kill of his own accord was that of Albert DeSalvo, the "Boston Strangler", who killed 13 women between June 1962 and January 1964, then went back to raping his victims but leaving them alive. DeSalvo claimed that he had felt shame after raping and strangling his last murder victim, 19-year-old Mary Sulllivan, because she had "treated him like a man" (i.e. like a human being). It could be said that DeSalvo had raped and murdered his way to a new level of maturity.

Is this what happened to the Wests after killing Alison Chambers in 1979? It is just conceivable. Stephen, Mae and Anne Marie all report that Rose West became a less brutal person with her younger children, and that the harsh regime at 25 Cromwell Street softened considerably during the 1980s. There are clear signs that Rose's personality, which had become so violent and uncontrolled under the influence of her husband, began to revert to the earlier mould of her childhood, when she enjoyed mothering younger children. "Mum got milder as she grew older, and the younger kids were spoilt compared to us." There are also signs that, as she reached her mid-30s, her sex drive began to diminish, and she began to long for a more normal life. Mae said: "(Mum) wanted more from him. He never used to take her out, although she wanted to go." We also have Mae's evidence that when Fred forced her to take up commercial prostitution in the mid-1980s, she objected strongly, and had to be bullied into it.

"Mum didn't really have any friends because Dad

wouldn't allow it. And if she found someone to have a cup of tea with, Dad would throw them out of the house. He didn't really want her to talk to anyone else. He wanted complete power over the house. Everyone answered to him. When Dad was home, that was it, Dad took over. As soon as he came home it was "I am here. I'm boss."

So West may just conceivably have been telling the truth when he claimed that he killed his daughter Heather because she was defying him. Any challenge to his authority threw him into the typical fury of the Right Man.

Heather, the first daughter of Fred and Rose West, had inherited something of her mother's intransigent character. Mae said of her: "You couldn't have cuddled her — she wasn't that sort of person." She smoked, drank, and when she was twelve years old, was arrested for shoplifting, although the case never came to court. As a child she had been cheerful and happy, and Anne Marie — who was delegated to look after her — said: "She was a delight — always smiling and cheerful." But as she grew into her teens, she became sullen, and began to bite her nails.

Heather's story resembles Anne Marie's in many ways. As a child she had been her parents' favourite — they called her "our love child." But from the time Heather was thirteen, her father pestered her about how soon she was going to lose her virginity. It was, he said, unnatural for a girl to remain a virgin that long — he claimed that if a girl was still a virgin at 16, she would be unable to have children. He also explained that a father was the right person to take his daughter's virginity, because an inexperienced boy "couldn't do it properly."

His advances became persistent, and Heather and Mae kept a lookout for one another as they were having a shower, in case their father tried to come in. Occasionally he succeeded, and reached round the shower curtain to fondle them. (The bathroom had no lock.) He made holes in their bedroom wall so he could watch them undressing, until — as Mae said: "My old bedroom looks like a sieve"; on one occasion when Mae was a little too forthright in rejecting his advances, he hurled a vacuum cleaner at her — Mae had to learn how to "reject him nicely." If he called either of the girls to his room, Heather or Mae took a brother or sister with them.

Some time in the summer of 1987, when Heather was sixteen, West entered her bedroom at night and forced himself on her. One day that summer, she burst into tears when talking to her friend Denise Harrison; Denise thought at first that it was because rumours about Rose's prostitution had reached the school, and the West children had become the butt of unkind jokes. When Heather told her that her father was having sex with her, Denise asked: "Have you told your mum?" Denise said that her mother did not believe her.

Denise told her own parents, Ronalzo and Gloria Harrison — the latter a West Indian, and a regular visitor at the home of the Wests. (Ronalzo Harrison had helped West find the money to put down on a mortgage of 25 Cromwell Street.) They apparently dismissed it as impossible.

In *Out of the Shadows*, Anne Marie explains that Heather had also been shocked and upset to learn that one of her close friends at school was, in fact, her half-sister — that the friend's father, a West Indian, was also the father of Rose West's three half-caste children.

The West Indian turned up at 25 Cromwell Street the next day, revealing Heather's indiscretion. As a result, Heather received a bad beating.

The conversation with Denise Harrison was undoubtedly one of the factors that led to Heather's murder a few weeks later. As far as Fred and Rose West were concerned, speaking to an outsider about what went on in Cromwell Street was an unforgiveable sin.

When Heather left school that June, her life became claustrophobic and grim. She became increasingly tense and nervous. She had been hoping to find a job, but jobs for school-leavers were scarce. But she had applied for a job as a cleaner of holiday chalets in Torquay, and — according to Graham Letts — suddenly became far more cheerful as she saw the prospect of escaping home and sex with her father.

She attended the third birthday party of Anne Marie's daughter Michelle on June 17, 1987, but stayed at the bottom of the garden, withdrawn and unsociable. Whenever Anne Marie tried to talk to her, Fred and Rose would quickly intervene.

Then, on the evening of June 18, 1987, someone telephoned Heather from Torquay to say that her application had been rejected. She spent all that night crying.

The following day, June 19, it was raining heavily. West decided to take the day off from his job — presumably because he was supposed to be working outdoors. When Stephen and Mae had gone to school, and Rose had returned from taking the younger children to school, Heather was alone in the house with them.

This was the day she disappeared. When Stephen and Mae came home from school, they were told that a woman had telephoned from the camp at Torquay and told Heather she could have the job after all. She had left, the Wests explained, with a lady in a mini. Later, this would be elaborated into the claim that she had left home with a lesbian in a blue mini. The Wests seem to have genuinely believed that Heather had lesbian inclinations, noting that she had never had boyfriends, and seemed suspicious of men. Rose may also have noted Heather's genetic resemblance to herself, and assumed that Heather had inherited her taste for her own sex.

Whatever happened to Heather, it seems certain that Fred West's story — that she had been defiant, and he had "wiped the smile off her face" — cannot be wholly true. Two short lengths of rope were found with the body, suggesting that she had been tied. Fibres of nylon carpet found trapped in the rope suggest that she was held down by one of them while the other tied her. According to Geoffrey Wansell: "Frederick West had abused his daughter precisely as he had his other victims, and for precisely the same reason — sexual gratification." And when West was asked whether his daughter might have been alive when her fingers and toes were removed — a charge he might have been expected to deny — he would only say: "I've no comment on that."

West dissected the body with a frozen-meat knife. Heather was decapitated and sawed up. Then the body parts were put into bin bags and put in a dustbin.

The basic motive for the murder was obviously their fear of what Heather might do now she was no longer at school. She had spent the previous night sobbing because the job had fallen through; her next step would probably be to run away from home (as she had once before). And sooner or later she would confide in some friend about the incest, as she had confided in Denise.

When Stephen came home, Fred asked him to help dig a hole in the garden, explaining that he was thinking of making a fish pond. Two days later, the hole was filled in again, and Stephen assumed that his father had changed his mind about the pond.

Oddly enough, Rose seemed genuinely upset that Heather had "run away", and cried a great deal — after all, Heather had been her first child, and had once been their favourite. However much she had come to dislike her later, Rose suddenly felt her loss.

One day soon after that, the telephone rang, and Rose answered it. Stephen was sitting nearby, and heard her say: "Hi, Heather, it's your Mum." As the conversation continued, Rose seemed to become upset, and said angrily: "You can't talk to me like that. I'll get your father." She called to Fred: "She's calling me every name under the sun — you can talk to her." Fred then picked up the telephone, and the argument continued, with Fred shouting: "You can't say that to your mother — she's brought you up." After a while he hung up, telling Rose "I've calmed her down."

A few days later, "Heather" rang again, and this time the conversation seemed more amicable, with Heather agreeing to write.

Stephen speculates that his parents persuaded some friend to ring up and pretend to be Heather. And he concludes correctly that this proved that Rose was aware that Heather was dead — she would hardly be deceived by another woman pretending to be Heather.

Mae notes: "After that Mum and Dad were much better parents. The abuse from Dad still went on but they bought us bikes, and Mum mellowed out. She wasn't nasty any more. After Heather went, she never hit me again. We could really see the change for the better ... " She assumed that her parents had realised that they were driving their children away with their behaviour.

Anne Marie was upset by her half-sister's disappearance, and went to the holiday camp in Torquay looking for her. When her father told her that Heather had quarrelled with the lesbian friend who took her away, and now had a job in a community centre near Gloucester, Anne Marie again tried to track her down; when she failed, Fred explained that Heather had already left.

It was not until five years later, in 1993, that Stephen and Mae began to wonder whether their parents had been responsible for Heather's disappearance. By this time, West had spent almost a year in custody for raping his daughter, and had escaped the consequences because Anne Marie decided to withdraw her own evidence about childhood abuse.

It was after the rape in August 1992, when Fred West was in prison in Gloucester, that the police began looking for Heather. Stephen says: "We would go with Mum to visit Dad in Gloucester prison ... and he started talking really strangely. He was crying and said that he'd done stupid things at night, when we were in bed. He said that he had done the worst crime that we could ever imagine. He became all pathetic, and for the first time in our lives said "I love you." It was the first time I had seen him cry. He seemed scared to death."

Understandably, Stephen and Mae began to wonder if "the worst crime they could imagine" was the murder of their sister. When he returned from the Birmingham bail hostel, West told them that he had seen Heather, but they were now inclined to doubt him. "Why would she contact him and not us?" They would talk in whispers about it until the early hours of the morning. "We thought that Dad might be capable of it, but that's different from believing that Heather had really been murdered."

They had watched a television programme called *Prime Suspect*, about a girl buried under a patio; it had a background of pornography. When the programme was repeated, they put it on, then watched their parents' reactions out of the corner of their eyes. It was clear that Fred and Rose found it fascinating — they watched with total attention — but without any sign of guilt. Yet even to watch a programme of this sort was unusual for the Wests, whose normal television viewing was confined to the news and sitcoms.

Stephen and Mae also made attempts to find Heather, writing to the Salvation Army, and to a popular television programme that specialised in finding missing relatives. But when finally they told their father they intended to go to the police station to report her missing, he made them sit down, and told them that Heather was involved in credit card fraud, and that if they pursued it, they would only get her into trouble." We sort of believed him, but after a while we stopped believing that he'd seen her."

Some time later, Stephen and Mae went to visit their younger brothers and sisters in care, and mentioned their suspicion that their father might be responsible for Heather's disappearance. One day, when the children were discussing this among themselves, they were overheard by their foster parents. This in turn was reported to Woman Detective Constable Hazel Savage, who decided to make an effort to persuade her superiors to look for Heather in the garden.

9
THE END

Fred West accompanied police to 25 Midland Road on Monday, March 21, 1994, to show them where he had buried Charmaine, but they were still too busy trying to establish the identity of the nine victims at 25 Cromwell Street to begin digging immediately. Besides, its present owner had to be moved out. Charmaine's skeleton was finally unearthed from under the kitchen extension nearly two months later, on May 5 — in pieces, like the others. Whether West had dismembered her, or whether the bones had become disarticulated when he moved them from the garden, was never established. Newspapers reported that radar had located five other bodies at Midland Road — a typical example of the sensationalism that the case continued to excite. No bodies, of course, were found.

West was also taken out to Fingerpost Field and Letter Box Field to try to point out the graves of Ann McFall and Rena West. But in the quarter-century since he buried them, the fields had changed — to begin with, the farmer had raised their level — and he was unable to point out the graves with any certainty. A mechanical digger sliced a huge trench, moving hundreds of tons of earth, but it was not until April 10 that the team in Letterbox Field found the skeleton of Rena West, together with a red toy boomerang.

In her safe house in Dursely, Rose West had been vigorous in her own defence, declaring through her solicitor Leo Goatley that she and Fred had led separate lives, and that she knew nothing whatever about the murders. She also declared that she would seek compensation for the damage the police had caused at 25 Cromwell Street.

As yet no one knew about her involvement in the rape of Caroline Raine or "Carol"; even so, few people could believe that she had lived with a mass murderer for 25 years without even suspecting it.

At first, Stephen and Mae stayed with her. Mae described the atmosphere as claustrophobic. Then, on Sunday, March 20, 1994, the *News of the World* carried a headline: "People May Not Understand, But I Still Love My Dad." The sub-heading read: "House of Horror son Stephen talks for the first time." In a three-page interview, Stephen revealed that his mother was a prostitute — at this time this was not generally known — and admitted: "it's hard to look at her, knowing the truth." He told how Rose had thrown him out of the house when he was 16, and how he was then only allowed to visit his home on invitation.

All this led to a headline a week later: "Horror House Mum Kicks Out Her Son", claiming that Rose West had thrown Stephen out of the safe house because he wanted to visit his father in jail. In fact she was furious that he had broken ranks and was talking to the press.

The police moved Rose and Mae West to another safe house behind the police station. "It was miserable there. We had no heating and no cooker. We were cold and hungry. The house really was a dump. It had dead flies on the windowsills, stone floors, and smelt of damp." But when a reporter saw Rose West out shopping, and followed her back, she was moved yet again, this time to a safe house in Cheltenham. Until then Rose had been an avid reader of every newspaper account of the case, and had watched every television news bulletin. But now newspapers were openly speaking of her prostitution, and when the story about Anne Marie's affair with Mike Spencer ("Come Home And You Can Sleep With My Daughter") made it clear she was a procuress too, she suddenly lost interest in the news.

She spent her days in her dressing-gown, smoking, and often in tears. Her sister-in-law Barbara, who visited her, told reporters that she did not want to speak about Fred. "She hates Fred now." With the typical irrationality of the Right Woman, Rose had decided that Fred was to blame for all her troubles, and that she was an innocent victim. She told her children that he had sold out to the Devil.

On April 21, 1994, Rose West was charged with raping an 11-year-old girl in the 1970s. Although she was not named, the girl was clearly Anne Marie. A coloured man, 67-year-old William Smith, was charged with her. A second man, Whitley George Purcell, 64, was also charged. Fred's brother John, a dustman, was charged with raping two underage girls in the 1970s. (The charges against all men were later dropped.)

Rose was refused bail, and taken to Pucklechurch Remand Centre, near Bristol. Her chief hope was still that lack of proof would prevent the police from charging her with the murders. But on April 22 she was charged with the murder of her daughter Heather, and of Lynda Gough. Lynda's mother June had told the police about her visit to Cromwell

Street, when she had seen Rose wearing her daughter's slippers, and seen some of Lynda's clothes hanging on the line.

Stephen and Mae had a reconciliation, and he and his girlfriend Andrea moved into the safe house. But when the address was read out in court it became uncomfortable. When Mae and Andrea were sitting outside on a hot June day a small girl on a bicycle rode past; then the child's mother grabbed her, shouting: "I told you not to go near those people." Stephen moved in with Andrea's parents, but was becoming increasingly explosive, and began hitting Andrea. When he threatened to kill both Mae and Andrea they had to send for the police.

It was not until June 7 that the skeletons of Anna McFall and her unborn baby were unearthed at Fingerpost Field.

On June 30 Fred and Rose West appeared in the same dock at Gloucester Magistrate's Court, charged jointly with nine murders; Fred was then charged with the murders of his wife Rena, and his daughter Charmaine. At this stage the police had not established that Fred was in jail when Charmaine disappeared. Fred touched Rose as he edged past her, but she resolutely refused to look at him.

It was Rose's rejection that Fred felt most strongly. He had lived up to his part of the bargain, done his best to shield her, insisted that she had played no part in the murders; yet she still sent him no message through the children who saw them both. He would not have expected her to make the slightest public acknowledgement of him, since her future liberty depended on convincing a jury that she had hated him ever since she learned he was a murderer; but it would have been easy to tell one of the children "Give him my love."

Stephen began paying regular visits to his father in prison, and what he heard shocked him. "I only made love to them when I thought they were dead." Stephen also states: "They had their nails pulled out and their fingers cut off while they were hanging up, and cigarettes stubbed out on them ... He didn't say why they were tortured, but they were ... He sexually assaulted them in the house, then he tied them up and tortured them, then he killed them and did whatever he did to them." Stephen believes that the bodies were taken elsewhere to be dismembered, and the lack of bloodstains at Cromwell Street seems to support that view.

When he asked his father why he had killed them West replied: "They all deserved to die. They were slags." This has been one of the basic justifications used by sex killers, ever since Jack the Ripper wrote: "I have a down on whores."

After these confessions West suddenly changed his story, and claimed that someone else had committed the murders. "He blamed everybody but the milkman", said Stephen.

On one occasion, while still in the police station prison, West confided that the police allowed him out for a smoke, and left him alone. He tried to persuade Stephen to help him break out by cutting the barbed wire.

What becomes very clear from these interviews is that West was not, in the strictest sense of the word, sane. The "monster" was behind bars, but he was certainly not fully aware of what he had done. This was the period when he told Stephen that he expected to receive ten years, and to be out in seven, and living back in Cromwell Street.

He also wanted to know if Stephen and Mae would return to Cromwell Street, and when Stephen said that he wouldn't be able to sleep at night, said: "Oh, but it's clean, isn't it?" When Stephen mentioned that Rose wanted to demolish the house West was upset; he wanted it to be kept standing as a monument — not to his murders, but to the work he had done to transform it.

Stephen found himself feeling sorry for his father. "He cuddled me a lot and said "I love you, son." Stephen admits that the hardest part was saying goodbye. "I wanted to stay and sit with him, see him through it."

Isa McNeill, Ann McFall's friend, had remarked that West was a Jekyll and Hyde. Now, in prison, Dr Jekyll was in charge. He even gave his son instructions about how Heather was to be buried, as if he was a mourning father. It was quite clear that he was unable to comprehend the enormity of what he had done.

In April, West was moved to Winson Green Prison, in Birmingham. He was a model prisoner, calling everyone "sir" — even his fellow-inmates. Some of them nicknamed him "Farmer Giles" because of his West Country accent; others asked if if he could make them a patio. But in fact he was steadily going to pieces. When Stephen came to see him he cried for the first twenty minutes. "The pressure in here gets to you." The other prisoners, he said, shouted at him and called him names. He was convinced that someone would seize the first opportunity to kill him. One prisoner had thrown a jug of boiling water at him. "Everyone in here hates me." He told Stephen: "If they take their eyes off me, I'll be gone."

On December 13, 1994, there was another court appearance, in which he was charged with twelve murders — now the murder of Ann McFall had been added. Once again, Rose ignored him. Stephen guessed that his father was more depressed than usual when he failed to telephone him before Christmas — West was allowed a telephone card.

At 11.30 on New Year's Day, when warders left Fred West alone in his cell at Winson Green prison, Birmingham, to eat his lunch, he plaited together strips of sheet from his bed, and hanged himself from a bar on the ventilation shaft above the door. He had waited until the holiday, when the prison would be understaffed, and then waited until lunch time, when there was a staff change-over. When found an hour later he failed to respond to all attempts at resuscitation. It seemed obvious that he had planned his suicide for weeks in advance.

He had left a note to Rose that read: "Happy New Year Darling. All my love, Fred West. All my love for ever and ever."

But far more significant is a note that was obviously written several weeks earlier. Although addressed to "Rose West, Steve and Mae", it is obviously written for Rose alone. He tells her: "Well, Rose, it's your birthday on 29 November 1994 and you will be 41 and still beautiful and still lovely and I love you. We will always be in love.

"The most wonderful thing in my life was when I met you. Our love is special to us. So, love, keep your promises to me. You know what they are. Where we are put together for ever and ever is up to you. We loved Heather, both of us. I would love Charmaine to be with Heather and Rena.

"You will always be Mrs West, all over the world. That is important to me and to you.

"I haven't got you a present. All I have is my life. I will give it to you, my darling. When you are ready, come to me. I will be waiting for you."

It looks as if he is telling her that he will commit suicide because without him there will be no case against her. Her "promises" are presumably promises never to confess, to insist that Fred alone committed the murders, and that she knew nothing about them.

Mae heard the news on the car radio as she was driving to Oxford to see a friend. She pulled in at a layby for half an hour and sobbed. Mae had left home in 1988, when she was sixteen, to prevent her father from carrying out the rape he had always hoped to commit. But when he was arrested for raping his daughter in 1992 Mae and Stephen had moved back in with their mother to give her moral support, and had stayed on after West was acquitted in June 1993. Mae records: "He treated me like a real person. He brushed past me a couple of times as though he was thinking of trying it on, but nothing more than that", and concluded: "It wasn't his fault. Sexually he was weird."

Anne Marie West made a suicide attempt after hearing the news.

The next day every newspaper carried a headline about the suicide — like "Death of a Monster" and "Happy Noose Year" — and page after page of material that was being reserved for after his sentence. The *Daily Star* carried six full pages, including a paragraph headed: "Anguish of Rose." "Rose West was said to be devastated after being told of her husband's death last night." But the *News of the World* that week told a different story: "I'm so relieved", says wife Rose." She had told her children: "He was evil. He should have died long ago", and added that she had prayed for his death."

Another newspaper stated that Rose had found God, having become a close friend of a nun named

Sister Mary Paul, who had been to see her on the day of Fred's suicide, and accompanied her in prayer.

Now there was speculation whether Rose would ever come to trial. Her solicitor Leo Gaotley declared: "The case against her was always flimsy, and now it is flimsier." One headline ran: "Will Rose West Stand Trial?"

The same issue of the *News of the World* contained a duplicate copy of a letter West had written to Stephen. "There no need to cum to see me you need to stay with andrea she needs all the help you can give her. And when she has the baby no working all day and night like I did or you cud end up in hear." He adds: "Have you seen May tell her dad woad lick to see her I ham her DAD and I love her. But she no that I forgive her for what she said to the police aboat me."

Several crematoria refused to accept West's body, and he was finally cremated on March 29, 1995, at Cranley Crematorium near Coventry.

In the New Year's honours list Hazel Savage was made a Member of the Order of the British Empire. But soon after West's suicide it was learned that she had been discussing a book on the case with a literary agent, and was thinking of asking a million pounds for it. The Police Complaints Authority launched an enquiry, and she was removed from the case. In the previous August, West's solicitor Howard Ogden had offered a book on West to a literary agent, including some of the pornographic tapes made at Cromwell Street. West had obtained an injunction preventing the book, and Ogden had resigned as his solicitor.

But would Rose West stand trial? That was what had to be decided at the committal proceedings, which began at Dursley, a small market town fifteen miles south-west of Gloucester, on Monday,

February 6, 1995.

The first stratagem of the defence, conducted by a junior barrister named Sasha Wass, was that newspaper stories about Rose West had destroyed any possibility of her receiving a fair trial. The magistrate, Peter Badge, rejected that view on the second day, and ordered the proceeding to continue. After that the prosecuting counsel, Neil Butterfield QC, began reading aloud the evidence against Rose West — how police officers looking for Heather West went to 25 Cromwell Street on February 24, 1994, and began digging, finally uncovering eight bodies. Then he moved on to the death of Charmaine, drawing the conclusion that Rose West had murdered her while Fred West was in prison, and that Fred West had buried the body outside the back door of 25 Midland Road.

He then went on to what was to be the first important evidence of Rose West's involvement in the later murders — the story of how Caroline Raine went to work for the Wests, how she was kidnapped, and then gagged while Rosemary had oral sex with her and Fred beat her with a belt, then raped her.

By that time Caroline's story had appeared in at least two newspapers, *The Sun* and *Today*, but they had taken care not to mention Rose as one of the participants. Now Neil Butterfield used Rose West's involvement as evidence of her "abnormal interest in young girls", and argued that she "obtained satisfaction from abusing a restrained and helpless victim."

There was worse to come. The story of "Carol" — referred to as "Miss A" because of a court order to protect her children — was told in detail, including the assault on the blonde girl with a vibrator and Fred's subsequent rape of her, as well as the anal assault on her with some hard object, and Fred's subsequent rape.

Anne Marie's testimony was also read out — how she had been taken to the basement by Fred and Rose when she was eight, and had a vibrator inserted into her, how Rose had apparently found her pain funny, how Rose had held her down while her father raped her, how Rose had forced her to perform cunnilingus, and how she had washed out her mouth with gargle afterwards. It all left no doubt whatever that Rose was a butch lesbian with a taste for sadism.

All this evidence was designed to show that Rose West was perfectly capable of sadistic sexual assaults on young girls, and that it was therefore extremely likely that she was present when the other victims were raped and murdered. As the week came to an end it was obvious that it had succeeded — by the time the evidence was over there was not a person in the courtroom who had any doubt that Rose West had taken an active part in the abduction and murder of the other girls.

During all this evidence Rose West sat looking quiet and demure, and occasionally raising her handkerchief to her eyes. But when a recording of her police interviews was played, with its foul language and general air of defiance, it became clear that she was now play-acting. Rose suddenly lost her self-restraint, and was taken off to the cells shouting abusively.

On Tuesday, February 14, the magistrate concluded that there was enough evidence to justify Rose West being sent for trial. He also added two more rape offences against young girls in the 1970s, committed with her husband. But the rape offences involving Rose and the two other men were dropped.

Not long after this Rose was transferred from the remand centre to the maximum security wing at

Durham jail, where Moors Murderess Myra Hindley would also shortly be transferred. Myra Hindley had been in prison since 1966 — almost thirty years — when she was 24. At 41, Rose could at least congratulate herself on having succeeded in staying out of jail far longer.

The main concern of the prosecution was that some newspaper would go too far in discussing Rose West's involvement, and give the defence another excuse to plead that a fair trial was impossible. Fleet Street editors were warned that from now on any indiscretions would be treated with the utmost severity. The result was a virtual news blackout on Rose West between February 1995, and her trial, which was set for October.

The trial of Rosemary West began at Winchester Crown Court on October 3, 1995; the presiding judge was Sir Charles Mantell. The prosecution was led by Brian Leveson QC, and the defence by Richard Ferguson QC. The trial was held at Winchester, rather than Gloucester, because of the suspicion that it would be easier to find an unprejudiced jury in Winchester.

Rose West had dressed "conservatively", in a black jacket, long black skirt, and white blouse, with a gold cross around her neck. She looked completely impassive, and totally unlike a mass murderess — which was no doubt the intention. It took only about five minutes to select the jury.

The defence knew, as Rose West knew, that if the jury was allowed to hear the same evidence as at the committal hearing — about Caroline Raine (referred to by her married name, Owens), Miss A and Anne Marie West — her conviction would be absolutely certain. Therefore it was of central importance that this evidence should be somehow excluded. In law, such evidence — of similar cases to the one under trial — is known as "similar fact evidence." The defence would argue that this evidence of other rapes was merely irrelevant and prejudicial. Richard Ferguson asserted that the evidence of living witnesses like Anne Marie West and Caroline Owens and Miss A could not be regarded as "similar" to evidence inferred from corpses; the two, he insisted, were quite different.

What he meant, of course, was that the evidence inferred from the corpses was more or less indisputable, whereas Anne Marie, Caroline Owens and Miss A might be telling lies for their own ends. In his book *She Must Have Known*, Brian Masters dots the i's and crosses the t's. He argues that Anne Marie had every reason to hate her stepmother, because Rose had come between herself and her adored father. In their trial for indecent assault on Caroline Owens in 1973, the Wests had not been accused of rape, and the only evidence that had survived from that period — a policeman's notebook — does not mention rape. Miss A had not told anyone of her alleged rape in 1977 until after the arrest of Fred West. But, says Masters, she had been proved a liar; after living with Rose West's brother Graham when she was fourteen, she had made false claims to be pregnant, and even sent him a picture of a baby she claimed was his. Since that time she had had several imaginary pregnancies, and had also suffered from hallucinations. Clearly, says Masters, she is unreliable and her evidence is suspect ...

Mr Justice Mantell understood all this perfectly well, and if he agreed, then it meant almost certainly that Rose West would be acquitted for lack of evidence to prove that she knew about the murders.

As it happened, he disagreed, pointing out that if

one of Bluebeard's wives had escaped to tell her story, then her evidence would certainly be relevant. In this case the disputed evidence showed that Rose West took an active part in stripping, tying up and sexually assaulting young girls, just as the dead girls had undoubtedly been stripped, tied up and sexually assaulted.

Richard Ferguson struggled on — for he knew that his whole case depended on this point. Evidence of murder is not the same as evidence of sexual assault, he protested. Perhaps the girls at 25 Cromwell Street were not sexually assaulted — just murdered.

Two days later — the court took a day off so Mr Leveson could celebrate Yom Kippur — the judge came back with his decision. The defence had lost. The Bluebeard's Wives who had escaped would be allowed to tell their stories, on the grounds that abducting and raping girls was similar fact evidence.

From that moment the defence must have known that Rose West was virtually convicted. The trial would last almost another seven weeks, but nothing was now likely to influence its course. Once the jury knew what Rose West was capable of, they would have no doubt that she had been there when Lynda Gough and Carol Anne Cooper and Shirley Hubbard and the rest had been abducted.

Even so, the trial was one of the most dramatic in British criminal history. The clampdown on Fleet Street meant that few members of the public had the least idea of what was involved — that Rose West had taken part in the kidnap and torture of young girls, on whom she forced her lesbian attentions. Brian Leveson spent two days telling the story of what had happened to a number of girls, beginning with Charmaine West, and continuing with the kidnap and rape of Caroline Owens. The Wests had allowed

Caroline to go home, but after they had to appear in court to answer for what they had done, they made quite sure that future victims were silenced.

Leveson admitted frankly that where the other victims were concerned the evidence was wholly circumstantial. There was not the slightest shred of evidence to prove that Rose West had been present when the girls were murdered. He might have gone on to add that if Rose West had been an ordinary housewife, engaged simply in looking after her children — even if she also treated them badly — and cooking the meals, she would not have been sitting in the dock. What made all the difference was that she was obviously as much a sex maniac as her husband ...

The purpose of the prosecution was now to build up a web of circumstantial evidence so tight and inescapable that no one could have the slightest doubt of Rose West's guilt.

The first witness was Rose's mother, Daisy, a white-haired old lady. She told how on the first — and only — occasion on which she had met Fred West he had boasted that he owned a string of hotels, which she knew must be a lie. After Rose had gone to live with West, against the wishes of her parents, she had left Fred and gone back home with four-month-old Heather. And during this visit her daughter had said: "You don't know him, mum. There's nothing he wouldn't do." And she thought Rose had added: "Even murder."

The point being made by the prosecution was clear: Rose knew that West had killed Ann McFall.

The next witness was Rose's sister Glenys, who described how Fred had told her that Shirley Robinson was pregnant with his baby. What was being established here was that Rose had good reason to want to get rid of her rival.

Next came Rose West's neighbour at Midland Road, Shirley Giles, who told the story of how her daughter Tracey had burst into Rose's kitchen to borrow milk, and found Charmaine standing on a stool, with her hands tied behind her, while Rose waved a wooden spon at her. After this Shirley Giles told how she had left Midland Road, and called back while Fred West was in prison — to be informed that Charmaine's mother had come and taken her away. The defence tried to argue that she had her dates wrong, and that when she wrote to Fred in jail, asking him to make her a model caravan, she had not mentioned her surprise that Charmaine was no longer there. Shirley Giles replied: "I didn't think of it."

It looked, on the whole — and in spite of the defence's querying of the dates — as if Charmaine had disappeared while Fred West was in prison.

The evidence of Elizabeth Agius was the most dramatic so far. With her gypsy-like shawl and long ear-rings, she looked — as Brian Masters commented — like a fortune teller. She was quite clearly nervous, and had been crying. It must have seemed to her an appalling ordeal — to be flown from Malta to appear before a defence whose purpose was to imply that she had been Fred West's mistress. The prosecution, of course, wanted her to tell how Fred and Rose had admitted that they used to "cruise" together in a car, trying to pick up young girls, and how Fred had shown her around 25 Cromwell Street and joked about his "torture chamber" in the basement. The defence immediately questioned this, on the grounds that Fred West had not built the trapdoor into the cellar until 1975, while Mrs Agius claimed she visited Cromwell Street in 1972. The implication seemed to be that she had remained intimate with the Wests for many years.

Next, Ferguson wanted to know if she had ever had sex with Fred West. She made the curious reply: "I don't know", then went on to deny it. Ferguson then wanted to know if she had not been in bed with both the Wests, and drew a furious denial. Ferguson went on to suggest that she had had sex with Fred West, while Rose was in hospital having Mae, and that Rose had returned unexpectedly and hammered on the bedroom door. Ferguson also revealed that Mrs Agius had told a policeman that she would deny the sex story if challenged in court, because it might destroy her marriage.

As Liz Agius crept out of court, looking tearful and traumatised, she must have felt that the ordeal had justified her worst fears. But the defence had really scored an own-goal, for it had made clear that Rose had given Mrs Agius drugged tea, and subsequently helped Fred strip her, carry her into the bed, and rape her. Since Rose was naked too, the implication was obviously that Rose was more than willing to help Fred subdue and rape women.

Next came Caroline Owens — whom Brian Masters describes as "formidably attractive", and "like a timid but beautiful bird that has just adjusted its plumage" — who described in detail her ordeal of December 1972: of being kidnapped and raped by the Wests. She was an impressive witness. And the defence had a difficult task on its hands trying to undermine her testimony. Ferguson set out to prove the apparently irrelevant point, that the assault could not have been as violent as she claimed, since she had had no bruises or cuts. He then went on to draw the admission that she had had sex with two lodgers at Cromwell Street, as well as a boyfriend. The aim, obviously, was to imply that she had been a willing victim of the Wests — which was clearly absurd, since she had reported it to the police. The judge, who was obviously getting rather tired of this apparently pointless attack on the character of the witness, intervened irritably when Ferguson began to question her about her dealing with the press, warning him that unless the latter could prove that it was relevant, he would stop it. Ferguson thereupon stated his point bluntly: that Caroline Owens had exaggerated her story to make it more dramatic, and therefore worth more money. The prosecution quickly disproved this point by pointing out that when she had made her first statement to the police no bodies had been found, and therefore she had no idea that her story might have commercial value.

When asked by Leveson why she had come to court she burst into floods of tears, and stammered: "Because I want to get justice for those girls who didn't make it, because I feel it was my fault." The outburst was so obviously sincere that it undermined the defence's allegations far more effectively than anything else she could have said.

After Caroline Owens, June Gough (Lynda Gough's mother) described how she had visited 25 Cromwell Street after her daughter's disappearance, and had recognised the slippers Rosemary West was wearing as Lynda's.

Another witness, Gillian Britt, underlined the point when she recalled how, as a lodger at 25 Cromwell Street, she had often seen Rose West going into her room after midnight with other men — occasonally three at a time. Sometimes Rose's "thumps, crashes, wails and shrieks" were so noisy that she had to turn up the radio to drown them out.

The defence interrupted to declare that all this was

salacious and irrelevant, but the judge did not agree. He was evidently anxious for the jury to grasp that life at 25 Cromwell Street was like a dramatised version of a pornographic novel.

The testimony of "Carol" — "Miss A" — provided the defence with another opportunity to try to prove that Rose West was not as black as she was painted. 'Carol' was obviously one of life's losers, pale, subdued and sad, and her voice was often inaudible. She told how she had been placed in care after sexual abuse by her father at home, how she had lived with Graham Letts when she was only fourteen — and he was nineteen — and how a middle-aged man who lived above them had blackmailed her into sex four times by threatening to report her. Then she told the story of her visits to Cromwell Street and of the evening when Rose West helped Fred to rape her. She also detailed some group sexual activity in which the third girl — Anne Marie — had taken part as though she were accustomed to it.

The defence cross-examined her about periods of psychiatric illness, and she admitted to having had hallucinations of a headless man, and a number of phantom pregnancies. Ferguson had no difficulty in establishing that she was an unreliable witness. Asked why she had not told anyone of the violence she had endured at the hands of the Wests, she answered: "Because I didn't know how to talk about it."

The defence told the judge: "Mrs West has no recollection of ever having met this woman."

But, as with Caroline Owens, Miss A was to have the last word. She said quietly: "I know what happened. It wasn't a fantasy, and they know it wasn't." And again all the defence's efforts to discredit her seemed to evaporate.

A middle-aged man named Arthur John Dobbs

told how after separating from his wife in the mid-1980s he had contacted a woman called Mandy through a contact magazine. Mandy was Rose West, and Dobbs was told to undress in front of Fred West. Fred then went out (undoubtedly to watch through the peephole), and Dobbs finally paid "Mandy" £10 for sex. He continued to see her for 18 months, even doing repairs to Fred West's car in exchange for sex. But when Rose West told him one day that Fred had been having sex with the children he reported it to the Social Services — who apparently took no action. ("The children" presumably refers to Anne Marie and Heather.)

On Wednesday, October 18, Anne Marie gave evidence. A heavily built woman, with eyes like her father, she spoke in a soft, shy voice that somehow left no doubt of her truthfulness. She described being deflowered with a vibrator at the age of eight, being raped by her father when she was nine, being forced to have sex with Rose's male friends when she was ten, and finally how she had become pregnant by her father when she was fifteen. There was something immensely impressive about her — as there was when she described the same events later on a television interview. Rose West often looked away as her stepdaughter told of beatings or other brutalities.

On the following day — Thursday, October 19 — the jury was taken to view Cromwell Street. Rose West declined to go on the grounds that she would find it distressing. The pressmen were also taken to see the empty house, the cellar with its chalk circles marking the sites of the bodies, and the holes cut in two beams. Children's graffiti on the walls reminded them that this had once been a bedroom.

On the night after her testimony Anne Marie attempted suicide with an overdose, and was taken to hospital. It was now Friday morning; later that day, when Anne Marie returned from the hospital, Richard Ferguson showed himself unusually gentle in his cross-examination, but brought up the fact that she had signed an exclusive contract with a newspaper. Ferguson attached great importance to this matter of payments from newspapers — since presumably it could imply that a witness might be prone to exaggeration — but it was clear that the judge was inclined to see this as an irrelevance.

On Monday the jury had their first chance to hear Rose West's voice — since she had so far sat without speaking. They also had the chance to see the other aspect of the demure widow whose eyes had been lowered through most of the proceedings; the police interviews that were now played on tape revealed her as coarse and foul-mouthed ("What do you think I am — a fucking computer?"). The courtroom heard her explaining that she had spent the night after Heather's murder with a coloured lover — on Fred's orders; she now thought Fred's intention in making her spend nights away from home was to commit rapes and bury bodies without her knowledge. Whenever faced with a question that might incriminate her, she claimed loss of memory. The tapes only reinforced the thoroughly unfavourable impression of her that had been conveyed by witness after witness.

The evidence given by Professor Bernard Knight was as gruesome as the court had been led to expect — particularly a photograph of the skull of Shirley Hubbard covered in tape, and with a tube inserted at the place where a nostril would have been. The pathologist explained that the tape-mask was slack because all the flesh had rotted away. After Professor Knight, the "tooth fairy" Dr David Whittaker demonstrated his technique of identification by superimposing a photograph of the victim on a photograph of the skull.

Detective Superintendent John Bennett, the final prosecution witness, described how he had "bugged" Rose's safe houses, hoping for an admission of her involvement, but how this had been unsuccessful.

There could be no possible doubt that the prosecution had presented an extremely powerful case. After hearing the testimony of Caroline Owens, Miss A and Anne Marie, nobody in court could have had the slightest doubt that the deaths of seven girls between 1973 and 1979 had been connected with sexual assaults, and that Rose West had taken an active part in those assaults. The problem was simply — as Brian Leveson admitted — that all the evidence was circumstantial. No one had actually seen Rosemary West assault or kill the victims.

That was the point made by Richard Ferguson when he opened his opening speech for the defence on Monday, October 30, 1995. He began by telling the jury "as loudly and as clearly as I can, that Rosemary West is not guilty." They would be wrong to assume that in this case the wife knew what her husband was doing. He mentioned that this did not apply in an unconventional household like 25 Cromwell Street.

He ended by springing a surprise on the jury. Rose West, he said, would now tell them she was innocent in her own words.

Brian Masters, who was at the trial, commented that they had all expected to hear a woman chastened and subdued. But although Rose West was chastened, she was certainly not subdued. Masters feels that deciding to call her as a witness was a major error. (It was rumoured she herself had insisted on speaking.) Although she attempted to present herself as deferential and respectful (calling the counsel "sir"), she was obviously belligerent and defiant.

Speaking in what one newspaper described as a "rich, expressive voice", and in a "brokenhearted tone", she told the story of her childhood, her job in a bakery in Cheltenham, and how she had been raped twice before she met Fred West. This may or may not have been true, but twice sounded too much of a coincidence, and inevitably raised the suspicion that it was a miscalculated attempt to gain the sympathy of the jury. When she told of her reaction of "shock, horror" when Fred West first invited her out it again seemed an oddly miscalculated reply — she might, after all, have felt surprise and irritation, but hardly shock and horror. "He was very persuasive", she went on to explain. "He promised me the world, he promised me everything. Because I was so young I fell for his lies ... He promised to love me and care for me and I fell for it. My mum had left me and my dad had abused my mum, and I just wanted someone to love me." The "abandonment" by her mother apparently meant the time when her mother had left Bill Letts because of his brutality, and Rose had preferred to stay with her father for reasons of her own.

When she met Fred West's children, she claimed, "I loved them right away. I felt sorry for them." Again that seemed a flat contradiction of the truth, which was that she treated them extremely badly, and finally murdered Charmaine.

Asked about Caroline Owens, she made an even greater mistake when she claimed that, try as she might, she could not recollect her. Since Caroline Raine had lived in her house for six weeks, and police evidence from 1973 demonstrated that she had been sexually assaulted by Rose, this had to be a preposterous lie. Rose West seemed to be doing her best to get herself convicted. Finally obliged to admit that she had been fined £50 for the assault on Caroline Raine, she insisted that she had "been fighting with Fred to stop it. I was as much a victim as Caroline herself."

When shown a photograph of Lynda Gough she denied calling at Lynda's home to take her out for a drink, and even denied that Mrs Gough had called at Cromwell Street looking for her missing daughter. It began to look as if Rose West was incapable of telling the truth even on the smallest point.

Asked about the £600 she claimed she had given Heather when she left home, she now recalled — for the first time — that it had come from her post office account. It seemed obvious that she had not "remembered" before in case the police checked on her story, and learned that she had never possessed an account with £600 in it.

Asked about Miss A, she at first declared that she had never met her, then made it obvious that this was a lie when she added that Miss A had been about to marry in 1977, displaying knowledge of a girl she claimed not to have met.

Cross-examining her, the prosecution had no difficulty in showing her to be a liar — for example, when she claimed that she and Fred led separate lives, when everyone who came to the house had been struck by their "togetherness." When Leveson pointed out that she had told her mother that Fred was capable of murder, she begged leave to explain, then told a story of how Fred had once tried to strangle her when she refused to sleep with other men. In view of her known nymphomania, this again sounded like a spontaneous invention.

It did not take Leveson long to discover that he

could extract damaging admissions from her by making her lose her temper. When she had three times denied killing Charmaine she was provoked into adding: "Where would I hide a little girl's body in 25 Midland Road?" as if this proved her innocence; it seems surprising that the jury did not chorus in unison: "Underneath the coal."

According to Rose, the discovery that her husband had murdered Heather had made her see him as "a walking figure of evil ... with horns and a satanic grin."

When she finally left the witness box, after three days, her credit was damaged beyond repair. She had succeeded in making a non-stop impression of dishonesty; even on matters that had been established beyond all doubt, such as her ill-treatment of the children, she used the same technique of blanket denial. When she returned to the dock the defence must have regretted calling her.

It was hard to see how the defence could present any evidence in her favour, since no one seemed prepared to say a good word for her. But Ferguson showed ingenuity in calling a series of witnesses who thought that Fred West — acting alone — might have tried to pick up the victims. Janette Clarke told how West had tried to persuade her to get into his car, and how she had been saved by her sister's intervention. Later, when she saw Fred West's face on television after his arrest, she had been shocked into dropping her tea. Other women then told how a man who might have been Fred West had tried to pick them up, but their descriptions varied so widely — one said he had a beard, another decribed his fair hair, and another his "staring brown eyes" — that the whole point — to prove that West tried to pick up women when he was on his own — was lost.

Now the defence decided to stake all on what was virtually its last card — to allow Fred West himself to proclaim his wife's innocence in court. It was in fact Rose's decision, and her counsels had warned her that if she insisted on these recordings being played the prosecution could then call further evidence in rebuttal; she had nevertheless decided to go ahead.

In the first of 4 tapes (out of a total of 145), Fred West decribed the murder of Heather — how Rose had left the house to get money for Heather, how Heather had threatened that if she was not allowed to leave home she would administer LSD to the children, and how Fred had squeezed her throat, then found she was dead. The story was quite clearly invention. If Rose had already gone to get money for Heather to leave home, then the matter must have already been decided, and there would have been no need to threaten to administer LSD to the children. The whole story of a tongue-tied, depressed sixteen-year-old girl uttering threats sounded absurdly implausible. And since the sole point of playing the tape was to enable the jury to hear West saying that Rose was out of the house at the time, and since the rest of what he said was so obviously untrue, the tape was damaging to Rose West's case rather than otherwise.

In the second tape Fred explains how to find the victims in the cellar, drawing a diagram, and then tells the police that he had had affairs with all of them, that all of them had told him they were pregnant, and tried to persuade him to leave Rose, and that he had killed them to save his marriage. He claimed that he knew Lucy Partington, the Exeter student, as "Juicy Lucy" because her vaginal juices were so plentiful, and that when she told him she was pregnant she had said: "I've been bloody looking for you — I want a thousand quid for an abortion." Again it was all so outrageously implausible that it made it quite clear that his sole aim was to exonerate Rose. (All the girls in the cellar, he declared on a third tape, were prostitutes.)

Lynda Gough's death, he claimed, was an accident. He and she had been enjoying bondage sex, and she had been hanging by her hands from a beam in the cellar; he went out to answer the door, and when he returned she had slipped and hanged herself.

But a statement made by West on April 19, 1994, was perhaps the most significant piece of evidence so far; Detective Constable Darren Law revealed that West had written a note that read: "I have still not told you the whole truth about this matter. The reason is that from the very first day of this enquiry my main concern has been to protect another person or persons."

In playing the tapes the defence had again shot itself in the foot. The prosecution was now allowed to call new evidence to rebut them.

First a probation officer named George Guest, who had interviewed West at the time of the rape of Caroline Owens, recalled that West had admitted freely that Rose was involved, and had taken a leading part. He quoted West as saying that Rose became a "raging queer" (i.e. lesbian) when she was not pregnant.

After this there was a statement from Lucy Partington's mother, demonstrating that she had been at university during the time West claimed he been having an affair with her; since no one had any doubt of this, it was virtually superfluous.

Detective Constable Steven Harris gave evidence that West had admitted in May 1994 that he was "protecting somebody." But since West also insisted that he had nothing to do with the murders, this claim apparently carried the implication that the "other person" was guilty. All this seemed to demonstrate was that he had moments in which he changed his mind about protecting Rose, and accused her of killing the victims. (He had told his son Stephen the same thing when he was in prison.) It seems to raise the interesting possibility that it was Rose who strangled the girls, in one of her sadistic fits of throttling.

Dr James McMaster, a psychiatrist who had interviewed West in August 1994, gave evidence that West had told him that Rose had been the one who had murdered the girls and buried the bodies, and that he, Fred, had nothing to do with it. But in cross-examination the defence succeeded in throwing doubt on McMaster's professional judgement by getting him to agree that, not long before West had hanged himself, he had arrived at the conclusion that West presented no danger to himself.

The letter to Rose that West had left in his cell after his suicide was read aloud in court. It not only seemed to demonstrate that West had entered into a pact to protect her — "Keep your promises to me. You know what they are" — but that he still worshipped her: "All I have is my life. I give it to you."

And now, at this late stage of the trial, some of its most dramatic evidence was to be presented. Janet Leach, the "appropriate adult" who had been called to serve as a witness at Fred West's interviews (and with whom the susceptible Fred had apparently fallen in love), now revealed some of the things West had confided in her.

He had told her in confidence that he had not been

speaking the truth during his police interviews. He had made a pact with Rose, under which he would take the blame for everything. When Rose was originally released West commented that the plan was working. Later, when she was re-arrested, he was obviously concerned that the police were getting too close to realising just how far she was involved. Therefore he had made up a tissue of nonsense in his interviews, just to confuse the issue.

Apparently West had also claimed that there were other people involved in the murders, including coloured men, Rosemary's father, and a man called Ralph. He also said that "a close relative" was with him when he picked up girls at bus stops.

But according to West, it was Rose who had committed the murders — he was always at work when Rose killed, although he sometimes helped dispose of the bodies afterwards. (He then contradicted himself by claiming that he knew nothing of the bodies until the police began digging in his garden.)

He told Janet Leach that Rose had murdered Charmaine while he was in prison in 1971, and that it was Rose who murdered Shirley Robinson and removed her unborn child from her womb.

Janet Leach had apparently found Fred's confidences so oppressive that, on the recommendations of the police, she was taken off the case, and subsequently suffered a stroke. But she had continued to speak to West on the phone, and to visit him occasionally. He had assured her that sooner or later he would tell the whole truth. So when he killed himself she felt betrayed and angry.

As the court returned from lunch Janet Leach turned pale, and collapsed; she was rushed to hospital. But the defence insisted that it was important to continue to cross-examine her, since what she had said so far was so damaging to Rose West. Moreover, she had been presented as one of the few witnesses who had had no dealings with the press, and he proposed to prove that this was untrue.

The cross-examination would not continue until six days later, on Monday, November 13, 1995. When Janet Leach came back into court she was in a wheelchair, and a doctor stood behind her. Ferguson quickly established that, far from avoiding press involvement, she had decided to write a book on the case, and a newspaper had offered £100,000 for serialisation rights. This, he suggested, was why she had kept up her acquaintance with West after she ceased to be his "appropriate adult" — she wanted to get more information for her book — for example, West had told her that he killed Mary Bastholm and buried her in a field. Ferguson also remarked on the fact that she had often seen West alone in his cell, and suggested that there had been some complicity between them. "Were you romantically involved with him?" By this time Janet Leach looked so pale and distraught that the judge became concerned. Her voice was scarcely audible. Her "demolition" by Ferguson was certainly the most remarkable court-room drama of the trial.

The court learned that one of the *Mirror* group of newspapers had paid her a number of considerable sums — £7,500 for the first option — and that her boyfriend had taken three of the payments so that they could not be traced to her. "It was his idea", whispered Mrs Leach, her voice little more than a croak.

Her evidence ended with even more drama when, in reply to a question by Leveson, she revealed that West had told her that there were twenty more bodies buried in fields. After this she was finally allowed to go.

The defence had scored a triumph. But could it possibly do Rose West any good?

In the final speech for the prosecution Brian Leveson left no doubt of how he saw the partnership between the Wests. She had always been the dominant one, the "strategist." And Fred West had presented her with the greatest possible gift: he had killed himself to try and save her. "The evidence that Rosemary West knew nothing is not worthy of belief. She says she saw nothing, she heard nothing, she smelt nothing. Well, she certainly said nothing."

There was little Richard Ferguson could do in his final speech for the defence except reiterate that there was not a shred of real evidence that Rose West had killed anyone. All the evidence showed that it was Fred West who was the depraved killer.

He even succeeded in disposing of one piece of evidence that seemed to show that Rose knew about Heather's murder — her charade on the telephone, pretending to talk to Heather. This, said Ferguson, was because of her shame that she had not kept in touch with Heather, and she had told lies to cover her shame.

He ended by comparing Brian Leveson to a mountain guide who had led the jury to a void, a gap in the evidence. He had invited them to jump across the gap. He implored them: "Ladies and gentlemen, don't jump, don't jump."

The judge's summing up — beginning on Thursday, November 16 — took three days. It was fair and balanced; he was obviously doing his best not to sway the jury with his own opinions. He warned them that they needed to keep cool heads and set aside all prejudice. Public clamour should be ignored. But he pointed out that if two people take part in murder, then both are equally guilty, no matter which of them actually did the killing. Rose's guilt did not depend upon her killing anyone; she would be just as guilty if she had simply been involved in some joint plan with her husband.

He then proceeded to an impeccably balanced summary of what various witnesses had said, with his own observations on their reliability. He laid particular emphasis on Shirley Giles's evidence about calling on Rose West while Fred was in jail, and hearing that Charmaine had been taken away by her mother. Anne Marie had also verified that Charmaine vanished while Fred was in jail. In other words, even if they might feel they had to acquit Rose West on the other charge, it seemed fairly certain that she had killed Charmaine.

On the question of witnesses being corrupted by the media, he commented only that the jury would have to make up their own minds about whether witnesses had been corrupted. The jury must have read this as advice that the defence's allegation that publicity had prevented Rose West from getting a fair trial should not be taken too seriously.

As far as Fred's confessions were concerned, he seemed to have no doubt that West had "rewritten the script" of the murders to "edit out the part" played by Rose.

Mr Justice Mantell finished his summary on Monday, November 20, 1995. At 3 p.m. the next afternoon, the jury returned. Asked if their verdict had been unanimous, the foreman said it had. When he announced a verdict of guilty on the murder of Charmaine, Rose closed her eyes and swayed slightly. On the next eight victims — from Lynda Gough to Alison Chambers — he explained that verdicts had not yet been reached. But on the murders of Heather West and Shirley Robinson, the verdicts were again guilty.

After a second night in a hotel, the jury came back with a question, the question, in fact, upon which the whole case had depended: was the absence of direct evidence an obstacle to bringing in a guilty verdict? To this Mr Justice Mantell's answer was no. A second question was really another version of the first: were they legally entitled to link together the presence of bodies at 25 Cromwell Street and the evidence of Caroline Owens and Miss A? To this the answer was yes. When she heard these answers Rose West must have realised that her last hope of being found not guilty of the seven sex murders had vanished.

The jury did not keep her waiting long; after only thirty-five minutes they returned to deliver a verdict of guilty on the remaining seven counts.

The judge told Rose West to stand, then told her that the sentence on the ten counts of murder would be life imprisonment for each. "If attention is paid to what I think, you will never be released. Take her down."

POSTSCRIPT

The West case is virtually unique in criminal history. There have been a few cases in which two sex-obsessed people have collaborated on murder, but nearly all of these involve two men — like the Hillside Stranglers, or the partnership between Henry Lee Lucas and Ottis Toole. The case of Gerald Gallego and Charlene Williams is one of the rare exceptions; but it resembled most other cases of "killer couples" in that the male was the dominant partner. When Fred West seduced Rose Letts in his caravan he was the dominant partner; but in the course of time Rose became "the boss." She demonstrated this when she chased Fred upstairs with a knife in August 1974 — when she was only 20 years old — and drove it into the bedroom door, almost severing her fingers. Rose was only just 19 when she told Fred that they had to "get" Caroline Raine, and presided over her kidnap and rape. And she was still 19 when she took part in the murder of Lynda Gough and Carole Ann Cooper, and 20 when she helped rape — and presumably kill — Lucy Partington, Therese Siegenthaler and Shirley Hubbard — she was a year younger than the first two victims. She was 25 when Alison Chambers, the last of the known "sex victims", was murdered.

Fred West differs markedly from most serial killers. Many possess a higher than average IQ — like Ian Brady, Ted Bundy and Dennis Nilsen, and most possess a higher than average dominance — like Paul Bernardo, Gerald Gallego and Hillside Strangler Angelo Buono. West was certainly below average intelligence, and did not strike his acquaintances as dominant. To explain his Jekyll and Hyde personality, his sudden fits of rage, and his total, undivided obsession with sex, we have to assume that his two motor-cycle accidents caused the kind of brain damage that — as we have seen — happened to many serial killers.

But what about Rose? How can we explain a 19-year-old girl taking part in two sex murders? It would be almost unbelievable, if it were not for the evidence of Caroline Raine and Miss A, which leaves no doubt that Rose was an aggressive butch lesbian.

If Rose had married the boy next door, there can be little doubt that she would have become a normal housewife — oversexed and overbearing, but otherwise normal. But she was oversexed; she had always been oversexed ever since she lost her virginity in her early teens. And, like most highly sexed people, she succumbed fairly easily to sexual temptation. Her brother said that after meeting Fred West, she became "sex mad."

That sounds an odd comment, since he admits that his sister had introduced him to sexual games when he was eleven. But it probably has a basis in fact. In spite of her father's reputed interest in children, she had been brought up in a home where any mention of sex was taboo. (Highly aggressive parents often have this "puritanical" streak; it is probably an aspect of their desire to control everything that goes on in the home.) And suddenly she was living with a man for whom sex was the sole purpose of existence, and who would have agreed with the Marquis de Sade that "a woman has no other purpose than to be fucked from morning till night." No wonder she became an instant convert to the gospel of promiscuity.

We must also take into account that almost anybody, no matter how naturally "virtuous", could be sexually corrupted, provided it happened gradually enough, and that this applies especially to the "dominant 5%", who are naturally highly sexed. We have all heard the story about the boy who, asked what he wanted to be when he grew up, replied "a sex maniac." And this is perfectly understandable. Boys grow up surrounded by pretty, fascinating little creatures in attractive dresses, and occasionally catch an exciting glimpse of their knickers when they bend over or sit with their legs open. By the time most males reach puberty — and often long before that — they experience a tingling energy in the genitals that seems to intensify when they look at a picture of a woman in her bathing costume or underwear.

Now the sexual ambitions of most pubescent males remain in the realm of imagination. But if some genie of the lamp offered to satisfy any of their wishes, a large percentage would immediately ask for the little girl next door to be conveyed into their beds in a state of drugged slumber.

In the world of reality, the sexual education of most young males is impeded by shyness, clumsiness and fear. But imagine what would happen if, when he was 15, a member of the dominant 5% met an attractive woman in her twenties who lost no time in seducing him, then offering to procure him school-girls, on condition that she was allowed to watch. Suppose also that she introduces him to oral sex, bondage and flogging. It is not difficult to imagine that by the time he is 16 he will be ready for rape, sadism and any other perversion she suggests.

Fred West gave Rose permission to indulge all her sexual desires. She must have felt like a child who has been taken into a pastry shop and told to eat as much as she likes. In no time at all she was — so to speak — sexually overweight.

The problem was that Fred was giving her permission to throw off all self-control. He himself had been a spoilt child, his mother's favourite, and now was turning Rose into a spoilt child. When she lost her temper and hit the children, he simply told her not to hit them where it would show. And when she went too far and murdered Charmaine he told her not to worry, and buried the body.

She had another characteristic of spoilt people; when something went wrong, she immediately looked around for someone to blame. It never occurred to her that she herself might be to blame for any problem. That was why she lashed out at the children whenever she lost her temper. And when, in due course their murders caught up with them she looked around for someone to blame, and fixed on Fred as the author of all her problems.

Fred was Rose West's Frankenstein; she was the monster he had created. But he was not a naturally dominant person; he had been a shy and unaggressive child, and by the time she was 18 — when they drugged Liz Agius — she was as dominant as he was. Rose had turned into a female version of her father; it was her sharp tongue and stern gaze that kept the children quiet. She had picked up Fred's foul language, and his favourite adjective "fucking", which she used in every other sentence. By her early twenties she struck most of their acquaintance as the more dominant of the two.

So they encouraged one another. Chance had brought together a sex maniac and a nymphomaniac, and they turned into a unique killing team.

All this raises again the question posed in the Introduction: how sex — which is essentially "love-making" — can turn into perversion, sadism and murder.

To begin with, we have to recognise that in sex we encounter what I have called "the paradox of the two realities." The world seems to have two faces. On the one hand, reality can seem dull, boring and all too solid. On the other, it can seem infinitely exciting and rich.

Everyday reality, with its demands for responsibility and hard work, confronts us when we open our eyes every morning. But in moments of affirmation and happiness we see "the other reality" — and it seems so self-evidently rich and complex that we feel we never want to die.

Now as a writer I pursue that vision of the "other reality" through ideas, through the mind. Beethoven pursued it through music, Einstein through science, Van Gogh through painting. But it is also clear to me that there are millions of people on earth, chiefly males, who have no capacity for abstract thought or music or art, and that they conduct their own version of the quest for "the other reality" through sex. The anonymous Victorian who wrote *My Secret Life* — who called himself Walter — was one of these; from the moment when in the nursery he lifted the bedclothes of his baby sister to see her genitals, he was obsessed by sex, and spent his whole life in pursuit of it. The subject fascinated him so much that he did his best to describe every sexual encounter of his life.

The first occurred when he was still a child with a

servant called Betsy. While she was sitting in a chair, he put his head in her lap and persuaded her to kiss him. Then — with some resistance from Betsy — he put his hand up her skirt. "Then came over me a voluptous sensation, as if I was fainting with pleasure, I seem to have a dream of her lips meeting mine, of her saying Oh! for shame! of the tips of my fingers entangling in hair, of the warmth of the flesh of her thighs upon my hand, of a sense of moisture on it, but I recollect nothing more distinctly."

He adds: "Afterwards she seems to have absorbed me." (He means obsessed him.) This is hardly surprising. The "voluptuous sensation, as if I was fainting with pleasure", was probably the most intense feeling he had so far experienced in his life. It is closely related to the feeling we experience on spring mornings, or setting out on holiday, or when some anticipated crisis fails to materialise. In such moments the world seems to become more real, and consciousness seems to achieve a new degree of completeness.

Anyone who experiences the "reality feeling" knows that it is the key to personal growth and evolution — the answer to the question of what we ought to do with our lives. So it is not surprising that Walter spent the rest of his life pursuing it with obsessive single-mindedness. This also explains what happened to those romantics of the late 18th and early 19th century — Goethe, Wordsworth, Coleridge, Shelley, Jean Paul, Novalis. Their "ecstasies" were not as crudely physical as Walter's, yet we only have to read Goethe's *Werther* or Shelley's *Alastor* to see that they had a strong sexual component.

Now "sex maniacs" like Fred West, Paul Bernardo, Gerald Gallego, are far too crude, too devoid of intellectual resources, for the romantic ecstasies of

Goethe and Shelley. Like Walter, they pursue the "voluptuous sensation " in the only way they know. Yet they are pursuing it for the same reason: an obscure feeling that it induces the "reality feeling", which is a key to personal growth.

The problem is that sex is the most dangerous way of trying to achieve personal growth, because the life force has mixed it so liberally with a strong sense of "magic", which, in the attempt at possession turns out to be an illusion. The attempt to possess a woman through an act of sex is as frustrating as trying to possess the scent of a rose by cooking and eating it.

In the *Symposium*, Plato makes a basic distinction between love and sexual desire. Sexual desire is an animal instinct; love is a relationship between two people whose personalities harmonise. But most sexual attraction takes place spontaneously, before there has been any interaction of personalities. Males like Fred West are simply responding to a "symbolic" girl in the way that a bull responds to a red rag.

Unfortunately, this "symbolic response", when combined with imagination, creates a mixture with far more explosive potential than "normal" sex between two lovers. The Marquis de Sade seems to have been the first writer to explore the incredibly powerful effect of purely symbolic sex, sex combined with imagination, and totally dissociated from personal response. Sade attempted to create a morality of symbolic sex, and his first step in this direction was to express his rebellion against his religious upbringing by declaring himself an atheist. This meant that he could concentrate on the symbolic aspect of sex without a feeling of "wrongdoing.". His next step was to create a kind of "superheated sex" in the way that 19th century engineers created superheated steam — sex without personal implications, sex as pure self-indulgence.

And here we can observe that strange transformation into violence that we discussed in the Introduction. His early books are simply about "forbidden" sex — sex between father and daughter or brother and sister. *Philosophy in the Boudoir* is simply a "dirty book", which alternates descriptions of sexual orgies with discussions on the non-existence of God. But then, as Sade allowed his imagination to dwell on innocence defiled, symbolised by a virtuous girl (Justine) whose misfortunes culminate in a series of rapes, the emphasis shifted from violation to cruelty. It is as if the act of penetration has become insufficient; he wants to flog and stab and mutilate. *Juliette* and *The 120 Days of Sodom* are orgies of cruelty and violence. It seems that in separating symbolic sex from personal sex he has started a chemical reaction that cannot be contained. Like sulphur and iron filings fusing together to make iron sulphide, nothing can halt the reaction once it has started.

It becomes possible to see how a man like Fred West is tormented by a perpetual sense of unfulfilment; he is like a man with a raging thirst who drinks a pint of ice-cold water and still feels as thirsty as ever. There had to be some way of making sex more exciting, more appropriate to the sheer violence of the desire that a male feels as he catches a glimpse of a woman taking off her clothes ...

It was inevitable that Fred West should feel there was something wrong with "normal sex", of the kind he experienced with Rena and Ann McFall. To begin with, he finds that making love in bed is unexciting compared to watching the same woman get undressed — and, moreover, that penetating her fails to bring the same intense excitement that he feels when watching her being penetrated by someone else.

At this point he meets a 15-year-old schoolgirl, Rose Letts, who satisfies his desire for "forbidden-ness", for she is not only willing to satisfy his abnormal sexual impulses — oral sex, sodomy, beating and being beaten — but is also happy to go to bed with other men and allow him to watch.

For Rose, Fred must have seemed like a dream come true. She was a nymphomaniac, and Fred was obsessed by sex. She was promiscuous, and Fred was perfectly happy to provide her with other men. She was fascinated by blacks, and Fred found her a series of black lovers, one of whom became the father of three of her children. Above all, she was a lesbian, and Fred had no objection to her taking female lovers, and actually finding them for her.

As far as we know, Liz Agius was their first venture into the realms of forbidden sex — forbidden in the legal sense. They both wanted to make love to her, so they drugged her, undressed her, and made love to her. It was a risk, of course. She might have been outraged when she woke up and rushed to the nearest police station. Fortunately, she did nothing of the sort — if the allegation made in court is true, it may have been because she found Fred attractive anyway.

The next venture into "forbidden" sex was the abduction and rape of Caroline Raine. Again, incredibly, they got away with it.

By now the house was full of lodgers — at first mostly male, at one point, five of them — later exclusively female. Fred was perfectly happy for Rose to sleep with the male lodgers, even though he was not allowed to watch. (Probably he listened outside the door.)

Then both felt it was time to repeat the experiment of "forbidden" sex. This time the victim was a girl who had already spent a great deal of time in the house, and who, like Caroline Raine, had slept with the male lodgers. Whether murder was intended to be part of the plan is unknown. Probably not — they were both attracted by Lynda Gough, and wanted her as a sex partner. And as she would be fairly easy to trace — as, in fact, June Gough did trace her — it would not be advisable to kill her. But both of them — as Mary Halliday later oberved — got their kicks from fear. Lynda would be taped down to the bed, flogged, raped by Fred, and subjected to oral sex and abuse with foreign objects. Fred would claim that he hung her by her hands from the beam in the cellar.

Here, in the privacy of his own home, with the victim taped down and gagged, Fred could afford to be carried away, to indulge his taste for flogging and drawing blood. With the victim tied up like a fly in a spider-web, he could play-act the part of the conqueror and tyrant — just as Paul Bernardo played "the king" with his victims. It was almost as if he was looking at himself in a full-length mirror. For half an hour or so, the ordinary, commonplace Fred West, the thief, the jailbird, the habitual liar, was Ivan the Terrible and Dracula rolled into one.

The composer Percy Grainger, who was also an addict of bondage and flogging, once wrote in a letter: "Everything that deals with sexual matters absolutely knocks me over. I love to simply wade and swim in a sea of overwrought, ceaseless sexual thought." This is precisely what Fred and Rose did. And wading in a sea of overwrought sexuality brought an intensified form of the "voluptuous sensation" that Walter sought.

The problem is that overwrought sexuality tends to be subject to the law of diminishing returns. To maintain the same level of feverish excitment, they had to move on from willing sexual partners — or more or less willing partners — to helpless victims.

As with Sade, what really excited their lubricity was the idea of innocence. This is why the Wests' next victim was the eight-year-old Anne Marie. Her rape with a vibrator, with her hands tied above her head, reveals that Fred and Rose were now thoroughly into "game-playing." The name of the game was power. One of Sade's favourite fantasies was of a young girl being held by her mother while he deflowered her. The Wests had gone one better, for the child was West's own daughter, and they were deflowering her to prepare her to become her father's mistress. They were wading and swimming in a sea of overwrought sexuality, and pitying the rest of the world for being so boring and unimaginative.

Now Fred could look at girls in a new way. He was not merely the Casanova, the seducer. He was their Master, the controller of life and death.

From then on the Wests were addicted to their game of Victim and Master. Oddly enough, they felt no particular guilt about it, for it was a game like bingo or pachinko, that could be left behind as they returned to ordinary life. But since it was illegal they had to keep the doors of 25 Cromwell Street closed to the outside world, and make sure that their children never spoke of what happened behind the doors. But then they had the perfect front. Who would suspect a landlord and landlady of being sex killers?

What should concern us most about the case of Fred and Rose West is that they remind us that we are living in a "society of complicity." The Victorians simply banned the subject of sex, and imprisoned anyone who tried to break the ban. There followed a long fight for "literary freedom" that ended in a new climate of tolerance, and the publication of *Ulysses*,

Lady Chatterley's Lover, My Secret Life and the works of de Sade.

The problem with a climate of tolerance is that it is practically impossible to stop it turning into a climate of complicity. The law may recognise the difference between *Lolita* and a paedophile video, but most people are bound to feel that the distinction is merely technical. This in turn encourages complicity among people who would normally feel guilt about their antisocial activities. The Mafia has always flourished — as the term *cosa nostra* implies — because its members can feel that they are not criminals but merely a part of a group that holds its own unorthodox views about law and order. Paedophile groups flourish because they lend one another psychological and moral support in their belief that there is nothing wrong with sex with children. One such group, which advertises on the Internet, defends paedophilia on the grounds that it was practised by the ancient Greeks.

Again it is virtually impossible to draw the line between intellectual and criminal complicity. In the 1980s, one group of British paedophiles made a habit of kidapping boys, subjecting them to gang rape, then murdering them. More recently, a Belgian paedophile, Marc Dutroux, has been arrested on suspicion of running a child pornography ring and being involved in the murder of fifteen children.

Killer couples like the Wests are a product of this "society of complicity", and form one of its most basic units. They are far more dangerous than the lone serial killer because they lend one another moral and psychological support, convincing one another that what they are doing is in some sense "normal." Unlike paedophiles, they are virtually immune to surveillance by the police, because they seem so ordinary. To the rest of the world Ian Brady and Myra Hindley, Gerald Gallego and Charlene Williams, Fred and Rose West, were indistinguisable from the couple next door. Which explains why the Wests were able to kidnap and murder for more than two decades.

One of the few crumbs of comfort for our "society of complicity" lies in the recognition that serial killers are basically self-destructive. As we read about Fred and Rose West, we can see that they behaved in a way that was bound to lead to disaster. Even in court, Rose West made no attempt to counteract the picture of her presented by the prosecution; with her lies and evasions, she seemed determined to convince the jury that she was the kind of person who deserved life imprisonment.

Another consolation lies in the fact that such killers are so rare. The chances of a sex maniac like Fred West meeting a nymphomaniac like Rose Letts must be a million to one.

Note: Fred West's brother John, 54, hanged himself from a beam in his garage on the evening of Thursday, November 28, 1996, hours before a jury was to return its verdict on whether he was guilty of repeatedly raping Anne Marie and "another girl", (presumably Mae). He was accused of raping and indecently assaulting the other girl at West's home in the late 1970s and early 1980s, when she was about eight. Anne Marie told the court that her uncle had raped her more than 300 times before she ran away from home at 15.

West had told Janet Leach that Rose's father William and his (West's) brother John had been involved in the murders. Geoffrey Wansel says that John had sex with Rose for many years.